THE THEORETICAL CONTRIBUTIONS OF KNUT WICKSELL

In the same series

Edited by Peter Bohm and Allen V. Kneese
THE ECONOMICS OF ENVIRONMENT

Edited by Jan Herin, Assar Lindbeck and Johan Myhrman
FLEXIBLE EXCHANGE RATES AND STABILIZATION POLICY

Edited by Steinar Strøm and Lars Werin
TOPICS IN DISEQUILIBRIUM ECONOMICS

THE THEORETICAL CONTRIBUTIONS OF KNUT WICKSELL

Edited by

Steinar Strøm
University of Oslo

and

Björn Thalberg
University of Lund

© *The Scandinavian Journal of Economics* 1978, 1979
English translation of "The Theory of Population, its Composition and Changes"
© Göran Ohlin 1977

Softcover reprint of the hardcover 1st edition 1979

All rights reserved. No part of this publication may be
reproduced or transmitted, in any form or by any means,
without permission

The proceedings on pp. 1–121 were originally published in
The Scandinavian Journal of Economics, Vol. 80, 1978, No. 2

First published in book form 1979 by
THE MACMILLAN PRESS LTD
*London and Basingstoke
Associated companies in Delhi
Dublin Hong Kong Johannesburg Lagos
Melbourne New York Singapore Tokyo*

British Library Cataloguing in Publication Data

Arne Ryde Symposium on the Theoretical
Contributions of Knut Wicksell, *Frostavallen, 1977*
The theoretical contributions of Knut Wicksell
I. Wicksell, Knut—Congresses
I. Title II. Strøm, Steinar
III. Thalberg, Björn IV. Lunds Universitet.
Institute of Economics V. "Scandinavian
journal of economics"
330.1   HB116.S

ISBN 978-1-349-04209-8   ISBN 978-1-349-04207-4 (eBook)
DOI 10.1007/978-1-349-04207-4

CONTENTS

Introduction *Björn Thalberg*	vii
The Life of Knut Wicksell and Some Characteristics of His Work *Torsten Gårdlund*	1
On the Relation between Keynesian Economics and the "Stockholm School" *Don Patinkin*	7
Keynesian Economics and the Stockholm School. A Comment on Patinkin's Paper *Bertil Ohlin*	17
Wicksell's Influence on Frisch's Macroeconomics in the Thirties *Jens Andvig*	20
Wicksell, Bowley, Schumpter and the Doll's Eyes *Ingolf Sthål*	40
Wicksell Effects and Reswitchings of Technique in Capital Theory *Luigi L. Pasinetti*	53
Wicksell and the Malthusian Catastrophe By *Richard Goodwin*	62
The Long-run Rate of Profit in an Economy with Natural Resource Scarcity *Michael Hoel*	71
Wicksell on the Currency Theory vs. the Banking Principle *Trygve Haavelmo*	81
The Long-run Demand for Money—A Wicksellian Approach *Lars Jonung*	88
Introduction to the Publication of Knut Wicksell's Lectures on the Economic Consequences of the First World War (1919) *Björn Thalberg*	103
The World War: An Economist's View *Knut Wicksell*	105
The Theory of Population, its Composition and Changes *Kntt Wicksell*	123

INTRODUCTION:
THE ARNE RYDE SYMPOSIUM ON THE THEORETICAL CONTRIBUTIONS OF KNUT WICKSELL*

In the Fall of 1977, The Institute of Economics at the University of Lund arranged a symposium on the theoretical contributions of Knut Wicksell and the subsequent development of his ideas by other theorists. The symposium was financed by the Arne Ryde Foundation.[1] The aim of the symposium was to examine the effects of Wicksell's ideas on the development of economic theory and to discuss the assertion that—fifty years after his death and seventy-five years after he was appointed Professor at the University of Lund—"Wicksell's message is not yet exhausted".

The symposium attracted about eighty participants, mostly teachers and research students from the Nordic countries. As the ideas of Wicksell generally lie within the core of economic theory, our discussions centered around fundamental questions of a purely theoretical nature. The seventeen papers presented at the meeting touched on many problems in a variety of fields.

The papers may by and large be divided into three groups. Some deal with questions concerning the history of economic thought, where the central theme is the relation between Wicksell and "the Stockholm School" on one hand and Keynesian economics on the other, with particular emphasis on Wicksell's influence on Keynes and Frisch. Torsten Gårdlund's eminent introductory talk on Knut Wicksell as a scientist may also be included in this context. A second group concerns problems in capital and growth theory, frequently based on Wicksell's model of wine (or wood) production and his analysis of the Åkerman problem. Third, some of the papers treat issues related to monetary theory, where a common point of reference is Wicksell's concept of the "natural" and "money rate" of interest and his analysis of the "cumulative process". Whereas a few of the papers are to be published elsewhere or as part of dissertations, the bulk of the papers presented at the symposium are included in this volume. The Institute of Economics at the University of Lund wishes to thank the editors of *The Scandinavian Journal of Economics* for devoting this special issue of the Journal to our Wicksell symposium.

Björn Thalberg
University of Lund, Sweden

---

* Held at Frostavallen, Sweden, September 19–20, 1977.
[1] Arne Ryde was a very promising young doctorate student at the Institute of Economics, Lund, who died after an automobile accident in 1968. We are most grateful to the founders of the Arne Ryde Foundation, who have made it possible for us to undertake arrangements such as this, for which our ordinary resources are not applicable.

THE LIFE OF KNUT WICKSELL AND SOME CHARACTERISTICS OF HIS WORK

Torsten Gårdlund

University of Lund, Lund, Sweden

Knut Wicksell was born in Stockholm in 1851. This was the year of the Great Exhibition in London, to which millions of people from the British Empire and the Western world came to admire the products of a rapidly expanding industrial system. In 1851 John Stuart Mill had married Mrs Taylor and with her begun to work on the radical pamphlets which were to be of a far greater general influence than the *Principles of Political Economy* he had recently published. 1851 was also the year of birth of two other members of the rising profession of economists—Böhm-Bawerk and von Wieser—and several of their colleagues-to-be were born only a few years earlier: Wicksteed, Edgeworth, Clark and Pareto.

Bearing in mind that Wicksell was not only to become an economist of great originality but also an agressively radical pamphleteer, it seems reasonable to ask whether there were traits in his family background which could explain his lack of adjustment to the conservative social and intellectual climate of his time. I have found no such traits. His family was fairly well-to-do, his father being a prosperous provision-dealer. Although his parents died when he was young—his mother when he was 7 and his father when he was 15—he received much understanding and encouragement from aunts, cousins and older sisters. He remembers his childhood as a reasonably happy one. However, at the age of 16 he was prepared for confirmation by an extremely severe and demanding pastor. He now became an ardent believer and was to live a pious life for a number of years, striving for spiritual improvement.

Wicksell began his university studies in Uppsala at the age of 18, studying mathematics, astronomy and physics. But he was not to receive his MS until 15 years later. In the meantime many things had happened to him.

In 1874 he lost his faith completely—under the influence of Renan, Strauss and other agnostic authors. Relieved from the bans of religion he began to take a more active part in student life and to read the new radical literature—Ibsen, Björnson, Strindberg.

A decisive influence was exerted on Wicksell and a group of liberal friends by a strange 600 page dissertation, *The Elements of Social Science. Physical,*

Sexual and Natural Religion. An Exposition of the True Cause and Only Cure of the Three Primary Social Evils: Poverty, Prostitution and Celibacy. The book, which had been published anonymously in England in 1854, was to be printed in 35 English editions and ten foreign-language editions, the Swedish one being published in 1879. The author was a Scottish medic by the name of George Drysdale, a friend of Charles Bradlaugh, the politician who openly fought for birth control, inspired by Malthusian ideas.

In 1880 Wicksell gave his first public lecture on Neo-Malthusianism in Uppsala, and he came to spend most of the eighties preaching its gospel and publishing a number of pamphlets. His first lecture was reprinted four times and sold almost 7 000 copies, which was enormous considering the time and country.

In 1885 a small inheritance made it possible for him to go to London, where he did some economic reading: the English classical economists, from Adam Smith to J. S. Mill, Jevons and Walras, Sidgwick and Goschen. But his thoughts mostly turned to matters of politics and social philosophy, and when he came back to Sweden he spent most of 1886–87 lecturing on Neo-Malthusianism and related subjects. His central theme was that overpopulation and not private ownership of the means of production was the cause of poverty. Late in 1887 he was given a travel grant from the Lorén Foundation—any *public* support being excluded by his radical ideas—and he now returned once more to London, where he spent most of his time talking to such reformers as Drysdale, Bradlaugh, Besant and Kautsky. He continued to Strasbourg where he listened to lectures which were mostly of a historical kind, and to Vienna where Menger also disappointed him by lecturing along the lines of the Historical School. He missed meeting Böhm-Bawerk but was able to procure his *Geschichte und Kritik der Kapital-Zins-Theorien*. He went back to Sweden via Berlin, where he stayed a few months in late 1888 and early 1889. There he found the newly published, second part of Böhm-Bawerk's *Positive Theorie des Kapitales* and "was soon lost in the book ... it came to me as a revelation ..."

Wicksell had now safely started on the road to economics—at the age of 37. In 1888 he had applied for a lectureship in Economics at the University of Stockholm but the post had gone to a younger man, Johan Leffler, who had no grasp of modern economic theory. Wicksell then asked the University for permission to give a series of lectures on the new marginal theory of value, but the petition was turned down. Instead, in the spring of 1889, he gave lectures on this topic at the Worker's Association in Stockholm. They were published four years later, with some minor changes, as an introduction to *Über Wert, Kapital und Rente*. During the early part of the nineties he made his first personal contribution to economic analysis by tackling the problem of the 8-hour workday. In several lectures and articles he demonstrated, by means of a marginal productivity model, that the final economic result of a shorter working week was likely to be a decrease in wages. Only a reduction in the population could produce an improvement in workers' incomes. In 1892 he published his first article in a scholarly periodical: *Kapitalzins und Arbeitslohn* in the *Jahrbücher für Nationalökonomie und Statistik*. Next year, in 1893, he published *Über Wert, Kapital und Rente*.

For his thesis, Wicksell chose a subject which could be treated without mathematics, the problem of the incidence of taxation. The public defense took place in Uppsala in the spring of 1895, and the book *Finanztheoretische Untersuchungen* was published the following year. As his work in value theory, this dissertation was inspired by his deep concern for social questions. "Now I shall set to work on my larger book covering the whole subject of taxes", he wrote to a friend in 1894. "I am truly shocked to see how confoundedly unfair it is to the little man—almost more than it used to be." As an example, the Swedish financier Marcus Wallenberg (1864–1943) had, in 1899, an income of 150 000 crowns and a net fortune of 1.4 million, not bad for a young man. His total tax on this income was not quite 2 100 crowns or 1.4 % of his income.

By the middle of the 1890's Wicksell's theoretical thinking had turned towards a new subject, the theory of money. He had previously been concerned with the problem of overproduction, Malthus' "general glut", which may explain why he now set out to clarify the problem of changes in general prices. During 1896–97 he worked on monetary problems, with economic support from the Lorén Foundation, and his *Geldzins und Güterpreise* was published in 1898. This time his choice of subject matter does not seem to have been directed by his social compassion. But during and after the first World War he certainly did apply his thinking on monetary problems to the politics of the day.

Geldzins und Güterpreise was received without enthusiasm, or even understanding. In the Swedish and Danish journals the reviews were remarkably ungenerous, and in Germany it was not reviewed at all. I have tried to show that Wicksell's new ideas were developed independently of Thornton's and Ricardo's short passages comparing real return to capital and monetary rates in the early years of the century; see Gårdlund (1958).

When he presented his theory before the Swedish Economic Association, not one single word was heard from this forum of economists, bankers and business men. The only exception to the disdain and silence he met was a review in the *Economic Journal* by C. P. Sanger, a lawyer-economist and, as it happens, a close friend of Bertrand Russell. Sanger wrote a warmly appreciative review and even suggested that the book be translated into English. Had the suggestion been followed *then*, instead of forty years later, international monetary theory would almost certainly have advanced more rapidly.

Wicksell's only meeting with Keynes took place almost 20 years after the publication of *Geldzins und Güterpreise*, during a trip to England made in 1916 on behalf of the Swedish *Riksbank*. About this meeting he wrote to his wife:

Then today I met Keynes and lunched with him at his club. We had a very interesting conversation. On some points he was not very well informed; for one thing he had no very clear idea of how to go about arranging a rational standard of value; thought it would be relatively easy, for instance on the lines suggested by Irving Fisher; he was very surprised when I began to criticize Fisher, but admitted straight away that my objections were valid.

On the other hand he has a good mind and, as I said, I gained much from our conversation; only wished it could have been longer; but he had to go as soon as we had finished lunch and had our coffee—however I walked with him to his barber's.

Wicksell was granted a chair in Economics in Lund in 1901, at the age of 50, and was promoted to full professor in 1903. In order to qualify for the chair, which belonged to the Faculty of Law, he first had to spend nearly two years cramming for a BL. The academic authorities had not agreed to a dispensation in spite of his qualifications as an economist.

During his 15 years at the University of Lund he wrote his *Lectures in Political Economy* and a number of articles in *Ekonomisk Tidskrift* and other journals. He also continued his radical lecturing and newspaper writing, on such subjects as population policy, free speech, the extension of suffrage, women's rights, antimonarchism, atheism, disarmament, and the appeasement of Russia—all extremely controversial subjects. In 1909 he was sentenced to two months imprisonment for "reviling and mocking God's holy word in such circumstances as to cause general offence", which he had done in a speech before an audience of young socialist clubs in Stockholm the year before. He served his sentence—thereby increasing his unusually thorough knowledge of social affairs.

After his retirement in 1916 he moved back to Stockholm and spent the last ten years of his life working on scientific articles and taking part in royal committees on monetary policy and public finance. He was also the center of the select Economists' Club in Stockholm—the GOM of Swedish Economics, admired and loved by all his younger colleagues with the possible exception of Cassel.

When Wicksell died in May, 1926 at the age of 74, the sad news made the first page of all the leading newspapers. In the elaborate funeral procession, similar to those usually reserved for statesmen, most of the 30 banners presented were red standards of the Labor Movement. Although he never was a Socialist, his memory was honored by all the main organizations of the Labor Party and the Trade Union Movement. Mr Wigforss, Minister of Finance in one of the early Labor governments, said in his speech that Wicksell, without being a party member, had been close to the hearts of the workers. He had enjoyed such confidence as rarely is given even to those who have totally accepted the pronouncements of the party.

*

Some of the characteristics of Wicksell's scientific work are reflected by the simple facts I have just mentioned. As the classical economists and many of the neo-classicals such as Jevons, Marshall and Wicksteed, Wicksell believed that economic analysis should be developed to elucidate contemporary social problems and should be made to serve "human progress". In spite of his criticism of the Historical School he often related his thinking to historical facts and problems. He warned against a purely abstract kind of analysis, and although originally a mathematician by training, he went out of his way to stress the limitations of mathematical treatment of economic problems. He also declared his admiration for economists such as Böhm-Bawerk and Marx who were able to tackle difficult analytical problems without any knowledge of mathematics. I think he rather exaggerated his criticism of mathematical expression in economics, but he did it out of consideration for those who lacked the proper training.

In his political struggle Wicksell often displayed a contempt for conservative and conventional opinions. But in the academic field he seldom gave vent to arrogance. In his bird's eye view on the development of the theory of value in the introduction to *Über Wert*, he shows great tolerance and understanding toward the generations which had grappled with the central problem without finding the solution that eventually was provided by the marginalists. As a scientist he was not only tolerant but also humble. He never bragged about his own performance, and when on some rare occasion he wrote degradingly about a fellow economist, it was about someone who had shown a *lack* of humbleness; Gustav Cassel is one example, Wilhelm Keilhau perhaps another.

If you were to count the number of words Wicksell had in print and include his pamphleteering, Wicksell had an enormous production. Even his books and articles in economics add up to a considerable life production. To a certain extent his political work and scientific work were mutually exclusive. But, as I have said, his political thinking played an important role in motivating his work as an economist.

In his most productive periods he actually worked simultaneously as a pamphleteer and a scientist. I think Wicksell's work gives good support to the rule that great academic contributions are made by those who work at their trade tenaciously, every day. With the exception of a few periods of inactivity and personal depression, Wicksell was at work at his desk for many hours every day. Most of the time he was actually *writing*: letters or newspaper articles, popular lectures or political speeches, and his masterpieces of economic analysis.

I had occasion, the other day, to go back to John Morley's great biography of Gladstone, which was published in 1903. Before forming his fourth administration in 1892, Gladstone spent a short holiday in Biarritz, accompanied by Morley. One of the general subjects they discussed and which Morley has reported verbatim was the possible benefit of *habitual* intellectual work. And in this context Gladstone asked a question: "How comes it that during the hundreds of years in which priests and fellows of Eton College have retired from hard work to college livings and leisure, not one of them has ever done anything whatever for either scholarship or divinity—not one?"

Knut Wicksell certainly was never able to retire from hard work to a life of leisure. Through his radicalism he had placed himself in a position where he *had* to work hard for his living, and this, I believe, kept him active and mentally fit—all to the benefit of his great scientific work.

References

Gårdlund, T.: *The Life of Knut Wicksell*.
 Uppsala, 1958.

ON THE RELATION BETWEEN KEYNESIAN ECONOMICS AND THE "STOCKHOLM SCHOOL"*

Don Patinkin

The Hebrew University of Jerusalem, Jerusalem, Israel

Abstract

The possible anticipation of the *General Theory* by the "Stockholm School" is a much-debated question in the history of modern macroeconomic theory. In order to deal with it, the distinctive analytical characteristic of the *General Theory* must first be defined. This is defined as the assignment of an equilibrating role to variations in output. The writings of Wicksell, Lindahl, Myrdal and Ohlin prior to 1934 are then examined, and it is shown that they do not contain such an analysis. Since Keynes developed the *General Theory* by the fall of 1933 at the latest, it is concluded that the "Stockholm School" did not anticipate him.

May I begin by expressing my appreciation for having been invited to participate in this Conference in honor of Knut Wicksell. I hope that without being presumptuous I can say that from the days that I first read Wicksell's works over twenty-five years ago, I have in a sense always felt that he was one of my teachers, one whom I should try to emulate not only in matters of economic analysis, but also in personal qualities. And what greater influence can a teacher have on a student?

This feeling only increases the trepidation with which I approach my talk today. For I come to talk to you not only about one of your greatest economists, but even more generally about a famous episode in the history of Swedish economics—and I do so without being able to read the original basic texts in Swedish. It would be bad enough if I were to do this in Israel or the United States, but to do so before a group of distinguished Swedish economists here in Sweden is really to be presumptuous. So let me at the outset ask you to forgive me if I say what I have to say on the basis of published and unpublished English translations of what seems to me to be the more relevant basic materials.

---

* I would like to thank my research assistant, Avraham Kamara, for his efficient help, and Susan Tamari and Beverly Griffith for carefully typing this paper through its various drafts.

This paper was written while I was a Fellow of The Institute of Advanced Studies at The Hebrew University. Work on it was aided by a grant from the Ford Foundation, administered by the Maurice Falk Institute for Economic Research in Israel. I am greatly indebted to all these organizations.

Let me also note that my paper today is essentially a report on work in progress. For as I shall indicate in the course of my discussion, there is some additional relevant material that I have not yet had the opportunity to study.

My subject today is one that was born with the *General Theory*. It gave its first lusty cry with Bertil Ohlin's well-known 1937 *Economic Journal* paper on "Some Notes on the Stockholm Theory of Saving and Investment". For many years afterward it remained dormant, but in the last decade—as a result of the monograph by Landgren (1960), the subsequent special issue of *Ekonomisk Tidskrift* (September, 1960), and the "anti-critique" of Steiger (1971)—it has become one of the most hotly debated issues in the history of modern macroeconomic theory.

On this issue there are two extreme, opposite views, with a whole range of views in the middle. At one extreme is what I shall for convenience call the "Myrdal view". I am not referring to Myrdal's 1933 chiding reference to Keynes' *Treatise* as an example of "the attractive Anglo-Saxon kind of unnecessary originality, which has its roots in certain systematic gaps in the knowledge of the German language on the part of the majority of English economists" (Myrdal [1933] 1939, pp. 8–9); for though I suffer from the same kind of "gap", I cannot but agree that Myrdal's criticism was well taken, and that the theoretical essence of the *Treatise* had been presented many years before by Wicksell. What I am referring to, however, is Myrdal's more recent remark that "the Keynesian revolution ... was mainly an Anglo-American occurrence. In Sweden, where we grew up in the tradition of Knut Wicksell, Keynes's works were read as interesting and important contributions along a familiar line of thought, but not in any sense as a revolutionary breakthrough." (Myrdal, 1972, pp. 4–5).

At the other extreme is what I shall for convenience call the "Cambridge view" and which I can best characterize as stating that "in the beginning" there was the *General Theory*, which developed in complete isolation from intellectual developments in Sweden; and then suddenly, after the publication of this book, came Ohlin (1937) and pointed out some *ex post* similarities between Keynes and Swedish economists. Let me regretfully note that this extreme view has recently received implicit support from Volume XIII of the Royal Economic Society's new edition of Keynes' *Collected Writings*, the volume entitled *The General Theory and After: Part I Preparation*, which is intended to present all the relevant materials, including correspondence, which led up to the *General Theory*. For this volume—which begins with Keynes' work on the *Treatise* in the late 1920's and ends with the publication of the *General Theory* in February 1936—does not contain any reference to any Swedish economists. Yet the fact of the matter is that there were contacts between Keynes and various Swedish economists throughout the late 1920's and early 1930's. Indeed, a serious omission from *JMK* XIII is the autumn 1934 correspondence between Erik Lindahl and Keynes which was reproduced by Steiger (1971, pp. 204–213), together with the draft of the note which Lindahl sent Keynes at that time.[1]

Besides this specific omission, the general methodological conception which guided the preparation of Volume XIII has, among other things, created the aforementioned false impression of the absence of intellectual contacts between Sweden and Cambridge. For as I have noted elsewhere (Patinkin, 1975, pp. 250–251), the editors of Keynes' *Collected Writings* have chosen to present the material not in the usual comprehensive, chronological manner, but by concentrating in Volume XIII all the materials that they felt relevant to the development of the *General Theory*. This has the advantage of producing a more readable volume; it has the disadvantage of imposing on the reader the judgment of the editor as to the relevance and significance of the documents from the period in question.

Thus Volume XIII does not reflect the famous Keynes–Ohlin reparations debate of 1929, where (as has been pointed out so often) there existed the paradoxical situation that it was Ohlin who was insisting on the necessity of taking into account the effect of an increase in "purchasing power" on demand —and it was Keynes who was persistently denying the validity of the principle that was to become the major one of his *General Theory*.

This, at least, is an incident with which we are in any event all acquainted. But what we are not acquainted with—or at least what I was not acquainted with until very recently—was the fact that there were other significant intellectual contacts between Keynes and Swedish economists in the early 1930's. This is a story that has now been related by Ohlin in a paper that will shortly appear. Here he tells us of his correspondence with Keynes during 1930 and 1931 in connection with the English translation of Wicksell's *Interest and Prices*; of his (Ohlin's) sending Keynes in 1931 (at the latter's request) an English translation of Wicksell's 1925 paper on "The Monetary Problem of the Scandinavian Countries";[2] and of his (Ohlin's) also sending to Keynes in 1933 a copy of his "Introduction" to the translation of *Interest and Prices*. Another possibly relevant event were the Newmarch Lectures which Ohlin delivered in London in 1932, at which time he also met Keynes. So contrary to the impression created by *JMK* XIII, there were many different ways in which Swedish intellectual developments might have influenced Keynes even during the period during which he was writing the *General Theory* (Ohlin, 1977, pp. 149–152, 161–163).

Obviously, to say that such intellectual contacts might have influenced the writing of the *General Theory* is not to say that they actually did—and it is to this basic question that I now turn. But in order to deal with it we must first

---

[1] This omission will be corrected in a Supplementary Volume to *JMK* XIII which will appear shortly. I shall return below to the nature of Lindahl's note.
[2] This subsequently appeared as an Appendix to the English version of *Interest and Prices*.

specify the nature of the distinctive contribution of the *General Theory* whose possible intellectual antecedents we wish to examine.[1]

Let me, then, emphasize at the outset that the distinctive contribution of the *General Theory* is not the advocacy of a policy of public-works expenditure as a means of reducing unemployment. The *General Theory* is, as its name indicates, a book concerned with theory. It contains practically no discussion of policy. And in particular it contains only brief, passing discussions of the policy of public-works expenditures. Furthermore, Keynes could not have seen the novelty of his book as lying in its advocacy of such a policy; for already in 1929, in his influential election pamphlet with Hubert Henderson entitled *Can Lloyd George Do It*, Keynes had been an outstanding and outspoken proponent of this policy. Correspondingly, the advocacy per se of public-works expenditure was not the purpose of the *General Theory;* rather it was to provide a theoretical underpinning for such a policy. It follows the much debated question of whether or not Swedish economists advocated public-works expenditures independently of Keynes is not one that is relevant to my purpose.

The distinctive contribution of the *General Theory* is instead best specified in the way Keynes himself did so in a letter that he wrote to Roy Harrod in August 1936, commenting on the latter's review of the *General Theory:*

... You don't mention *effective demand* or, more precisely, the demand schedule for output as a whole, except in so far as it is implicit in the multiplier. To me the most extraordinary thing, regarded historically, is the complete disappearance of the theory of demand and supply for output as a whole, i.e. the theory of employment, *after* it had been for a quarter of a century the most discussed thing in economics. One of the most important transitions for me, after my *Treatise on Money* had been published, was suddenly realising this. It only came after I had enunciated to myself the psychological law that, when income increases, the gap between income and consumption will increase,—a conclusion of vast importance to my own thinking but not apparently, expressed just like that, to anyone else's. Then, appreciably later, came the notion of interest being the measure of liquidity preference, which became quite clear in my mind the moment I thought of it. And last of all, after an immense amount of muddling and many drafts, the proper definition of the marginal efficiency of capital linked up one thing with another. [*General Theory*, p. xv, italics in original; see also *JMK* XIV, p. 85.]

Now, Keynes himself had attributed the notion of the marginal efficiency of capital to Fisher; he did this somewhat late in the process of writing the *General Theory*, but then he did so generously. And in any event, Swedish economists who had been brought up on Böhm-Bawerk's productivity theory of capital as expounded by Wicksell, did not need Keynes for this notion—though they may have benefitted from the precise way in which he (following Fisher) defined it. Insofar as the theory of liquidity preference is concerned, this is clearly a contribution of Keynes, but it is one that he had already developed

---

[1] In the following three paragraphs, I have drawn freely on material in my *Keynes' Monetary Thought* (1976; referred to henceforth as *KMT*), and in a subsequent essay (1977).

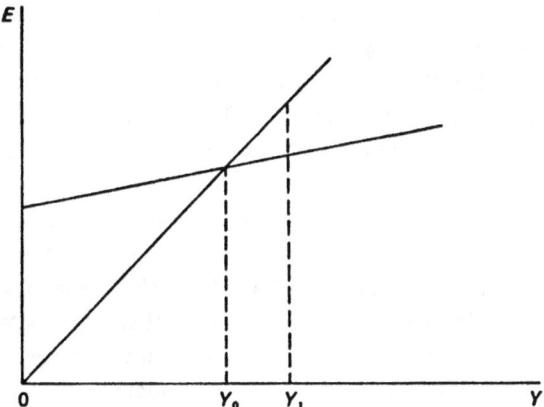
Fig. 1.

considerably in the *Treatise*. To this I should in the present context add that the dependence of the demand for money on the rate of interest was recognized by Wicksell, but not in a way which to my mind constitutes recognition of the theory of liquidity preference in the full sense of the term.

This leaves the theory of effective demand as the distinctive analytical contribution of the *General Theory*. In order to explain what I mean by this theory, let me make use (as Keynes unfortunately almost never did) of a diagram. In particular, in terms of the familiar diagonal-cross diagram, it is not only that the intersection of the aggregate demand curve, $E = F(Y)$, with the 45° line determines the equilibrium level of output Y_0, but even more so that changes in output themselves act as an equilibrating device. This is, if the economy is out of equilibrium at, say, Y_1, then the reduction in income and hence output itself will bring the economy to equilibrium by its influence on consumption or saving, depending on which language you wish to use. Correspondingly, as we have just seen, Keynes emphasizes that a critical part of his analysis is the assumption that the marginal propensity to consume is less than unity. For if the marginal propensity to consume were equal to unity, you would not have any equilibrating device; for then as income would decrease, spending would decrease by exactly the same amount, so that any initial difference between aggregate demand and supply would remain unchanged. This is the crucial point of the *General Theory*: the theory of effective demand as a theory which equilibrates aggregate demand with supply by means of automatic changes in the level of output.

To me, yet another contribution of the *General Theory*—which was made explicit by Hicks' IS-LM interpretation—is the analysis of macroeconomic phenomena within a Walrasian general-equilibrium model, even if only a very simple two-equation one (*KMT*, pp. 98–101).

And now let me go on to say—and this essentially summarizes the rest of this paper—that I do not think that the foregoing theory is to be found in the Swedish literature before the *General Theory*. For in general this literature continued to be primarily concerned with the analysis of movements of price, with the analysis of output being derivative from this. Correspondingly, this literature does not contain the basic Keynesian notion of the equilibrating role of changes in output.

Thus let me begin with Wicksell and remind you that the subtitle of his *Interest and Prices* is "A Study of the Causes Regulating the Value of Money". Correspondingly, as I contended many years ago (Patinkin, 1952; see also 1965, Note E: 4), Wicksell's purpose is to explain the dynamics of the quantity theory in an economy with a banking system. In such a system, an increase in the quantity of money affects prices by first depressing the market rate of interest below the natural one, thus leading to an increase in the demand for investment goods, hence to a state of excess demand in the markets, and hence to a rise in prices. And this is a "cumulative process" in the sense that prices will continue to rise as long as the market rate lies below the real one—even if the market rate should not continue to fall any further. This process will come to an end, says Wicksell, when as a result of the loss of reserves caused by the internal drain generated by the price rise, the banks will raise the market rate to equality with the natural one.

That, it seemed and seems to me, is what Wicksell's *Interest and Prices* and subsequent *Lectures* are all about. And, frankly, it has always been a matter of concern to me—an indication that perhaps I did not fully understand Wicksell —that Swedish economists have always seen much more in his writings, as witnessed for example, not only by Myrdal, but also by Ohlin's "Introduction" to the English translation of *Interest and Prices*. But may I be permitted to suggest that though Swedish economists should presumably know best about Wicksell, they are also likely to be more susceptible than an outsider like myself to read into his works more than they contain—just as many English economists have done with respect to Keynes.

Some of this reading-in, however, occurred in the late 1920's and early 1930's, and so is relevant for our purposes in that it represents Swedish economics as it existed before the *General Theory*. This is the impression I have from reading the works of Lindahl (1939 [1929]) and Myrdal (1939 [1933]) that have been translated into English.

Thus let me concentrate in particular on Myrdal's *Monetary Equilibrium*, which (according to his Preface) represents with minor changes his 1933 German essay. In this work Myrdal expounds not only his ideas at the time, but also those of Lindahl. One of the things that emerges from this exposition is that whether or not this motif is explicit in Wicksell's writings themselves, Lindahl and, following him, Myrdal interpreted these writings as representing an analysis of the existence of discrepancies between aggregate demand and aggregate supply, and hence as representing a pathbreaking escape from Say's

Law (Myrdal, 1939, pp. 19–21). But in contrast to Keynes' *General Theory*, Lindahl and Myrdal applied this discrepancy to an analysis of changes in prices, and not (directly) to changes in the level of output. Indeed one need only read Myrdal's analysis of the effects of an increase in savings on the economy (1939, pp. 106 ff.) in order to see how far he was at the time from the conceptual framework of the *General Theory*.

On the other hand, it is also clear from Myrdal's book—as it was in Ohlin's subsequent 1937 article as well—that Swedish economists were well ahead of Keynes on the whole question of the analysis of anticipations and the consequences of the emergence of discrepancies between such *ex ante* anticipations and the corresponding *ex post* quantities.

Much the same comments can be made for Ohlin's 1933 *Ekonomisk Tidskrift* article "Till frågan om penningteoriens uppläggning"—"On the Question of the Method and Structure in Monetary Theory."[1] Here once again the emphasis is on the analysis of the price level, and not directly of the level of output. Furthermore, I do not think that Ohlin contends otherwise in his forthcoming essay (1977)—though he does express the view that the distinction between the analysis of price and the analysis of output is not the crucially significant one that I together with other students of Keynes' writings, such as Axel Leijonhufvud, consider it to be (Ohlin, 1977, p. 153).

Let me now return to that unpublished note which Lindahl sent Keynes in 1934. Once again, the direct concern of this note is the determination of prices, and not output. Indeed, in his accompanying letter to Keynes, Lindahl himself relates the argument of his note to the fundamental equations of Keynes' *Treatise*, which were in turn concerned with prices.

My final bit of evidence is also from Lindahl, this time from his 1953 *Ekonomisk Tidskrift* article on Keynes which appeared a year later in English. In this article Lindahl describes the analytical novelty of the *General Theory* in much the same terms as I have described them above, and does not even hint at any claim that these novelties were already part of the Swedish tradition. Of course, this difference between Lindahl and Myrdal may reflect the different personalities of these two individuals. And yet I think there is more to it than that.

In particular, Lindahl refers to

... Keynes' most original contributions to economic theory: the introduction of the volume of employment and, also, national income as a regulator for the establishment of equilibrium between saving and investment; the determination of the interest level with the aid of the liquidity function and the connected division of the volume of money into active and nonactive balances—a good move, at least from a pedagogical point of view; and generally his determination of monetary and real magnitudes in one system. (Lindahl, 1954, p. 167.)

---

[1] I have read this in an English translation prepared by Moshe Apelblat, a student at the Hebrew University of Jerusalem.

And in accordance with what has already been noted above, his criticisms of Keynes is directed at the latter's inadequate treatment of anticipations, and of the crucial dynamic role of discrepancies between *ex ante* and *ex post* quantities.

And this is the way I too would summarize the relationships between Keynes' *General Theory* and Swedish economics: I do not believe that the latter anticipated the fundamental analytical novelty of the *General Theory;* but it did supplement it in a most valuable way by means of its *ex ante – ex post* analysis. Thus it is no accident that this analysis, as applied to the accumulation of inventories, rapidly became an integral part of the standard exposition of the dynamics of the Keynesian system.

Let me in conclusion emphasize that I have here examined the Swedish literature available to me only through 1933. It is possible that the literature of 1934–1936 contains developments closer to the *General Theory*. But even if it does, it clearly could not have influenced Keynes; for as I have shown elsewhere (1976, p. 79), Keynes developed the basic analysis of the *General Theory* by the fall of 1933 at the latest. Hence the most that might be attributed to the "Stockholm School" is a simultaneous discovery of the principle of the *General Theory*. But whether or not it actually did make such a discovery is a question that I hope yet to study.

References

Hicks, John R.: Mr Keynes and the 'Classics': A suggested interpretation. *Econometrica* 5, 147–159, April 1937. As reprinted in *Readings in the theory of income distribution*, by the American Economic Association (Blakiston, Philadelphia, 1946), pp. 461–476.

Keynes, John Maynard: *A treatise on money, vol. 1: The pure theory of money*. 1930. As reprinted in Keynes' *Collected writings*, vol. V.

Keynes, John Maynard: *A treatise on money, vol. II: The applied theory of money*. 1930. As reprinted in Keynes' *Collected writings*, vol. VI.

Keynes, John Maynard: *The general theory of employment, interest, and money*. 1936. As reprinted in Keynes' *Collected writings*, vol. VII.

Keynes, John Maynard: *The general theory and after, part I: Preparation*. Edited by Donald Moggridge. Vol. XIII of Keynes' *Collected writings*, 1973.

Keynes, John Maynard: *The general theory and after, part II: Defence and development*. Edited by Donald Moggridge. Vol. XIV of Keynes' *Collected writings*, 1973.

Keynes, John Maynard: *Collected writings*. Macmillan, for the Royal Economic Society, London, 1971–1973.

Keynes, John Maynard & Henderson, Hubert: *Can Lloyd George do it? An examination of the liberal pledge*. 1929. As reprinted in Keynes' *Collected writings*, vol. IX, pp. 86–125.

Landgren, Karl-Gustav: *Den 'nya ekonomien' i Sverige: J. M. Keynes, E. Wigforss, B. Ohlin och utvecklingen 1927–1939 (The 'New Economics' in Sweden: J. M. Keynes, E. Wigforss, B. Ohlin and the Development 1927–1939)*. Almqvist & Wiksell, Stockholm, 1960.

Lindahl, Erik: *Studies in the theory of money and capital*. Unwin, London, 1939.

Lindahl, Erik: On Keynes' economic system. *Economic record*, part I, May 1954, pp. 19–32; part II, Nov. 1954, pp. 159–171.

Myrdal, Gunnar: *Monetary equilibrium*. W. Hodge, London, 1939. Translated from the German edition of 1933, which is a revision and enlargement of the original Swedish version of 1931.

Myrdal, Gunnar: *Against the stream. Critical essays on economics.* Pantheon, New York, 1972.

Ohlin, Bertil: 'Till frågan om penningteoriens uppläggning', (On the question of the method and structure in monetary theory). *Ekonomisk Tidskrift* 35 (2), 45–81, 1933.

Ohlin, Bertil: Some notes on the Stockholm theory of saving and investment. *Economic Journal* 47, part I, March 1937, pp. 53–69; Part II, June 1937, pp. 221–240. As reprinted in *Readings in business cycle theory*, by the American Economic Association (Blakiston, Philadelphia, 1944), pp. 87–130.

Ohlin, Bertil: Some comments on Keynesianism and the Swedish theory of expansion before 1935. In *Keynes, Cambridge and the general theory: The process of criticism and discussion connected with the development of the general theory.* Edited by D. Patinkin and J. C. Leith (Macmillan, London, 1977), pp. 149–165.

Patinkin, Don: Wicksell's cumulative process. *Economic Journal* 62, 835–847, 1952.

Patinkin, Don: *Money, interest, and prices.* Row, Peterson, Evanston, Ill., 1956. 2nd ed. Harper & Row, New York, 1965.

Patinkin, Don: The collected writings of John Maynard Keynes: From the *Tract* to the *General theory. Economic Journal,* 85, 249–270, June 1975.

Patinkin, Don: *Keynes' monetary thought: A study of its development.* Duke University Press, Durham, 1976.

Patinkin, Don: The process of writing the general theory: A critical survey. In *Keynes, Cambridge and the general theory: The process of criticism and discussion connected with the development of the general theory* (ed. D. Patinkin and J. C. Leith), pp. 3–24, Macmillan, London, 1977.

Steiger, Otto: *Studien zur Entstehung der neuen Wirtschaftslehre in Schweden: Eine anti-Kritik.* Duncker & Humblot, Berlin, 1971.

Steiger, Otto: Bertil Ohlin and the origins of the Keynesian revolution. *History of Political Economy* 8 (3), 341–66, Feb. 1976.

Uhr, C. G.: Economists and policymaking 1930–1936: Sweden's experience. *History of Political Economy* 9, (1) 89–121, 1977.

Wicksell, Knut: *Interest and prices: A study of the causes regulating the value of money* (1893). Translated by R. F. Kahn. Macmillan, London, 1936.

Wicksell, Knut: *Lectures on political economy.* Translated by E. Claassen, and edited with an introduction by L. Robbins, vol. 1, *General theory* (1901); vol. 2, *Money* (1906). Routledge, London, 1935.

Wicksell, Knut: The monetary problem of the Scandinavian countries. *Ekonomisk Tidskrift* (1925). English translation by Mrs H. Norberg published as Appendix to Wicksell's *Interest and prices* (1936).

KEYNESIAN ECONOMICS AND THE STOCKHOLM SCHOOL. A COMMENT ON DON PATINKIN'S PAPER

Bertil Ohlin

Stockholm, Sweden

Professor Don Patinkin expresses the view that the real content of Keynes' theory of effective demand in the *General Theory* was his development of a theory for underemployment equilibrium and its application to explain the relationship between fluctuations in investment and changes in employment. The mechanism relating the two was the change in the total volume of output brought about by a variation in investment, which subsequently gave rise to a change in the volume of savings, whereby the latter came to equal the size of investment.

My view on this is the following: If investment falls to a size smaller than the volume of saving, which is compatible with full employment, then a situation of full employment will degenerate into a contraction. There will be lower employment and lower aggregate income. As Wicksell's theory of the cumulative process demonstrated, *the investment will, however, also decline in most cases*. It is quite possible that a stable equilibrium will never be reached. The rate of interest may fall step by step. This may stimulate investment and causing it first to coincide with, and then to exceed the lower volume of savings, which was the immediate consequence of the fall in employment and output, which was caused by the original fall in investment. The output will start growing!

The advantage of a theory of an underemployment *equilibrium* seems to lie chiefly on the pedagogical side. But, other more dynamic theoretical constructions can convey the same insight into the causal connections and perhaps, in a more realistic manner.

Keynes' very simple model rests on the simplifying assumption that the volume of investment will not be affected by the decline in output! He also seems to assume that the depression tendency will not bring about any essential decline in the rate of interest. In most cases these two assumptions are unrealistic, particularly the former. Wicksell's cumulative process with some further precisions is more realistic, when variations in output and not only in prices are considered as causes of changes in total income.

Patinkin's answer to my remarks may be roughly summarized as follows: The essential part of Keynes' theory is that there is a "feed-back" from the change in employment and total income setting off changes in the volume of saving. Keynes also explains when, or rather, *under which conditions* the downward development will stop.

My answer to this is that it depends on how investment and savings react. This was a problem discussed by the old theory of business cycles. In the Stockholm theory we took account of a "feed-back" from changes in total output to changes in saving but also changes in investment and, *thereby* in employment. See papers by Myrdal (1933) and Ohlin (1933) and (1934).

I also want to emphasize the usefulness of the *ex-post* concepts of saving, investment, employment and output etc. in a sequence analysis, as defined in Stockholm. The *ex-ante* concepts deal with *plans* based on earlier experience and on opinions about the future. Such plans aim at actions which are often incompatible with one another. Planned investment can very well be different from the planned saving.

The sequence analysis must analyze what has happened during a terminated period and demonstrate *how savings have become equal to investment—ex-post*. For they are always equal in a retrospective analysis. It is self-evident that one has to explain *how* this situation is brought about. The instruments are the reactions of savings and investment and total output to the process. There is no other way. Naturally, realised saving may differ from planned saving and as well as realised investment from planned investment. *The existence of a "feed-back" from changes in total output—caused by primary investment or savings variations—is an inevitable conclusion inherent in this conceptual apparatus in a sequence analysis.*

It is self-evident in the Stockholm discussions that a decision to increase savings, which is not accompanied by a decision to increase investment, would bring about a decline in the total demand and output, and possibly in prices. The problem was handled in this way in my paper on monetary theory, which was circulated among some Stockholm economists towards the end of 1932 (Ohlin, 1933). It was also made clear in Myrdal's German paper on monetary theory published in the volume edited by Hayek (Myrdal, 1933). In the earlier Swedish text he was exceedingly critical of period analysis and used a *point equilibrium analysis*.

As Patinkin and others have got the impression from the preface to Myrdal's *Monetary Equilibrium* published in 1939, that it was in all essentials a translation of the Swedish and the German version of Myrdal's text, I want to point out that, as mentioned in Myrdal's preface, three chapters had been added. There was also a considerable revision of the text in another part of the book.

Patinkin is obviously quite right in regarding Lindahl's paper in the *Ekonomisk Tidskrift*—Lindahl (1953)—as lending support to his impression that the Stockholm theory before 1936 contained no explicit reference to "feed-back" from variations in total output to changes in savings and to a stop in the "process" when savings and investment were equal.

Evidently, Lindahl had at that time forgotten that he and Myrdal and myself had followed a line of reasoning which implied this feed-back process, and that I had explained it in the paper of 1933 and more fully in my report in the spring of 1934. (I refer also to my letter to Lindahl who asked for comments on his survey of concepts, printed in Steiger's paper in *History of Political Economy* (1976).)

Patinkin is justified in maintaining that the reasoning presented in Stockholm in 1932 and in 1933 concentrated attention more on price level alterations than on changes in the total volume of output and employment. The latter were, however, taken into account in our 1933 papers. In the reports about Measures against Unemployment, published by Myrdal and myself in the first half of 1934, it was self-evident that attention was given to employment variations. I refer to the following pages (pp. 12–14, 19–23) in my report (Ohlin, 1934).

Keynes' model was static and "stopped" when the output variation had made savings coincide with investment. This was the equilibrium position. The character of the preceeding transition is not clear unless the terms "unintentional" savings and investment are used. In a more dynamic reasoning with equality of *ex-post* savings and ex-post investment *in all positions*, there is no need of such equilibrium constructions.

I maintain that the fundamental apparatus, which has to be used when the aim is to give a picture of the causal relations between savings and investment variations and consequent *price* development, is largely the same as the apparatus used when one is interested in changes in the volume of employment and *output*. Even if less attention is given to comments on employment variations when price changes are in focus—which was the case in 1933—the formal mechanism will be the same. In 1934 as much attention was given to employment as to price variations. The task was to indicate how different kinds of economic policy could be used to bring about an increase in employment, and to some extent to preserve a stabilisation of employment on a desired level. Keynes' oversimplified, but pedagogically brilliant, model of underemployment equilibrium based on some unrealistic assumptions, was in my opinion less suited for an analysis of the effects of different kinds of monetary policy, public works, subsidies and tariffs, for in such cases as a rule both prices and output volumes varied during the process.

When I met Keynes in 1935 in Belgium, where he gave me a general impression of his new theory, I observed, that there was a great deal of similarity with the theory which the Stockholm economists had developed on the basis of Wicksell's theory. I made a brief outline of our reasoning with cumulative processes and employment variations. Keynes' comment was that this sounded very much like the kind of reasoning he himself had been working with a couple of years earlier. He believed, however, that he could convey the essential ideas in a simpler way. He had, therefore, decided to use a different model in his analysis of employment variations.

It is widely known that Keynes (1936) radically simplified his theory in several respects with exactly this aim in mind. He did the same thing with the marginal productivity of capital; and also in his price analysis in abstaining from the use of the theory of marginal revenue which his pupil Mrs Joan Robinson had done so much to develop in the course of 1932 and to publish in 1933 at the same time as Chamberlain published his famous work in USA.

Permit me to add that in the British literature about economic policy in the late 1920's—already in the *Yellow Book* of 1928 but more clearly in "Can Lloyd George do it?" in the following year—it was explained that in a country with large unemployment, it was not necessary to wait for an increase in savings before starting a large increase of public investment financed through borrowings. The process of expansion brought about by the latter would increase national income and saving. Kahn (1931) made it still clearer in his famous paper. To what extent the theoretical development in Stockholm in 1930-1934 was helped by these expositions, is impossible to say. But I am quite convinced that the books, pamphlets and articles written by Keynes and Henderson as well as by Robertson and Hawthrey in the 1920's, stimulated the thinking in Stockholm in a general way, encouraging an attack on the problems of unemployment with the aid of a theory for a policy of economic expansion. Elsewhere I have given some reasons for the belief that, on the other hand, Wicksell influenced the thinking at Cambridge in 1931-33. See Patinkin & Leith (1977).

References

Kahn, R.: Home investment and employment. *The Economic Journal*, 1931.
Keynes, J. M.: *General theory*, 1936. See Ch. 21.
Lindahl, E.: Om Keynes' ekonomiska system. *Ekonomisk Tidskrift*, pp. 186–222, 1953.
Myrdal, G.: Der Gleichgewichtsbegriff als Instrument der geldtheoretischen Analyse. In *Beiträge zur Geldtheorie* (ed. F. A. Hayek), pp. 427–36, 1933.
Myrdal, G.: *Monetary Equilibrium*, 1939.
Ohlin, B.: Till frågan om penningteorins uppläggning. *Ekonomisk Tidskrift*, 1933. ("On the question of the method in monetary theory".) An English translation will appear in *History of Political Economy*, in the autumn of 1978.
Ohlin, B.: Penningpolitik, offentliga arbeten, subventioner och tullar som medel mot arbetslöshet, 1934. See pp. 12–46.
Patinkin & Leith, eds., *Keynes, Cambridge and the General Theory*, 1977.
Steiger, O.: Bertil Ohlin and the origins of the Keynesian revolution. *History of Political Economy*, vol. 8. no. 3, 1976.

WICKSELL'S INFLUENCE ON FRISCH'S MACROECONOMICS IN THE THIRTIES*

Jens Andvig

University of Oslo, Oslo, Norway

Abstract

The part of Frisch's work during the thirties which is best known is his econometric and methodological research. But he also participated actively in the Norwegian debate on the economic depression. Partly inspired by this debate, Frisch made some studies in macroeconomics and monetary theory which may still be of interest. Some of these studies were influenced by Wicksell. This paper constitutes a survey of some aspects of Frisch's macroeconomic thinking and traces the influence of Wicksell, primarily in order to elucidate Frisch's research from this period. Frisch's interpretation of the cumulative process is also presented.

> "There is probably no other economist who has had so much influence on my thinking, at least not in monetary theory"
> Frisch on Wicksell; Frisch (1951), p. 2.

I. Introduction

To evaluate the research performed by an economist by considering only some aspects of his theories, chosen more or less by chance, might easily be misleading. A clear picture of Frisch's aims, his general approach or paradigms and his methods and allocation of working time is important when evaluating Frisch's own macroeconomic analyses and the possible influence of Wicksell on different aspects of his work.

II. Frisch's Macroeconomic Research Program, 1930–1936

II.1. *Choice of Problems. The "Frischian" Paradigms*

Frisch's interest in macroeconomics in the thirties was, naturally, greatly influenced by economic development itself, with a high rate of unemployment

---

* The research connected with this article was financed by The Norwegian Research Council for Science and the Humanities.

and low agricultural prices as the most acute problems. It became important for him to elucidate these phenomena in order to urge politicians to implement correct solutions.

An overriding aim in all of Frisch's work was his wish to make economics a precise and quantitative science and to combine theoretical speculation with observation, developing the necessary statistical methods along the way. The necessity of theory in this combination was, in my opinion, what Frisch regarded as the most important thing he ever learned from Wicksell. Wicksell's solution of the Gibsons paradox might be mentioned in this context. In the thirties, Frisch's macroeconomics did not live up to these ideals and remained primarily on the speculative level, although he did work hard to develop a national accounting system for Norway during the latter part of the thirties. But as is well known, he concentrated his macroeconomic research on methodological problems.

In his general approach, Frisch emphasized that the economic system had to be studied as an entity. This was due to the relationship between markets and to the way individuals and institutions reacted to each others' actions. An implication of the latter attitude was that the transition from micro to macro could not be made by means of simple analogy deductions, for example by using a Marshallian representative individual in studying the economic depression. Even if Wicksell rarely studied depression problems, it is tempting to draw a parallel with Wicksell's work in monetary theory. Many examples can be found where Wicksell criticized economists who had made mistakes by moving from micro to macro too easily, such as his critique of the Banking School's treatment of interest as a cost element, his critique of the view that technical progress generates a tendency toward falling prices, etc. It is evident that Wicksell was very conscious of this point:

> In economics false conclusions are all to easily drawn by applying to a national, or to an international, economy knowledge which, before further examination is undertaken, is appropriate only to the private economy from which it is derived (Wicksell, 1936, p. 85).

During the depression many dramatic economic changes occurred almost simultaneously. Although Frisch discussed many other aspects, he was perhaps most interested in the workings of the monetary system and its relations with other parts of the economy. The total economic result of individuals' actions differed, depending on how they were related by the exchange system and how the banking system worked. It was therefore not possible to disregard— as Keynes did later on in his *General Theory*—the workings of the banking system when explaining the economic crisis. Here too we find a close parallel to Wicksell, who thought the behavior of the banks was decisive for the problem he was primarily interested in, i.e. movements in the general price level.

II.2. The More Technical Aspects of Frisch's Research Program

Frisch's analyses of the economic crisis are dispersed in works with dissimilar features, from journalistic writings, speeches and official committee reports to rigorously constructed dynamic models. The approach Frisch usually used in his scientific writings may be summarized briefly as follows.

First he constructed a model which was explicit, dynamic and determinate, with a small number of variables. He then inserted some "reasonable" guesses as to the numerical values of the parameters and examined how the model behaved when it was "shocked". The main idea underlying this procedure was Frisch's belief that the economic system "in itself" generated regular and damping oscillations, but when it was exposed to shocks such as war and political strife, it exhibited irregular, but not necessarily damped fluctuations. This was an idea, by the way, which he attributed to Wicksell (1933a, p. 28).

In the last stage of his approach, Frisch tried to decompose the (calculated) time series for the variables into sinus components with different wave lengths. Frisch did not, as one might expect, try to estimate the parameters in his different dynamic systems empirically. That was a job at which Tinbergen was the first to make a serious try.

Frisch did not attempt to integrate his different macrodynamic models. His work in this field thus remained incomplete and impressionistic, regarded as efforts to analyze the economic depression (but not as methodological studies).

III. Frisch's Analysis of the Economic Depression[1]

Frisch grouped the phenomena he thought most important in relation to the economic depression into three clusters.

The first was the skew distribution of income among members of different production sectors. In a simple model he showed that a fall in one sector's prices might result in a drop in this sector's income and an increase in unemployment, but not necessarily in a reduction in income in the other sectors. Here Frisch had in mind the effects of the fall in agricultural prices.

The second—and more important category according to Frisch—was the skew distribution of income between capitalists and the working class. He also studied this situation by means of a simple model. Although it seems that

---

[1] Frisch's great methodological interest often poses a problem with regard to discussing his own view of the causes of the economic depression. It is clear that this methodological interest often dominated his choice of models; it also made his scientific work unnecessarily difficult, and often somewhat dull, reading. Even when he started to discuss important, "burning" economic questions, he had a tendency to delve into numerical details. As a result, in the thirties, it was mostly statisticians and mathematicians who could (or cared) to follow his work to the end. This, happened, I think, with his important article, "Circulation Planning". Fortunately, in a letter to a Norwegian parliamentarian, Jon Sundby, he expressed directly his views regarding what he considered the most important clusters of causes. The disposition in this section is based on this letter (5-4-1935).

he intended to construct a Kaleckian-like model stressing the effective demand consequences of income distribution between classes, he ended up with a purely falling rate of profit type of explanation for fluctuations in output.[1]

Neither of these two explanations of the depression-generating mechanism was visibly influenced by Wicksell, but in his study of a third class of mechanisms, Frisch was evidently inspired by Wicksell's work in monetary theory. Frisch regarded this third class of phenomena, which he called "the incapsulating phenomena', as the most important of all the processes which constituted and explained deep depressions. In "Circulation Planning" (1934b) he gave it the following description:

One very important aspect of the disastrous effects during great depressions by the present organization is what might be called the *incapsulating phenomenon*. It manifests itself in various forms and in different fields, but its nature and deplorable consequences are always the same: It is fundamentally connected with the fact that modern economic life has been divided into a number of *regions* and *groups*.

Under the present system, the blind "economic laws" will, under certain circumstances, create a situation where these groups are forced mutually to undermine each other's position. Each is forced to curtail the use of the goods produced and the services rendered by the other groups, which in turn will cause a further contraction of the demand for its own products, and so on (1934b, p. 259).

Frisch discovered the "incapsulating phenomena" in a wide range of processes, often only casually related. He detected it in the depositors' run on the banks. He saw it when bankers tried to call in loans in order to improve their liquidity, which only resulted, according to Frisch, in a reduction in the stock of deposits and a worse liquidity position.

More fundamental was the "incapsulating" process which could be observed in the exchange system and in the relation between saving and investment in a capitalistic economy. As already noted, Frisch viewed the division of the economy into separate groups as fundamental to the possibility that an "incapsulating" process might be triggered off. Applied to the study of the circulation of goods among individuals and groups, this signified that the monetary mechanism, especially in its function as a means of circulation, was important. Money could easily mediate multilateral exchange, and thus make possible the division of producers and consumers into largely autonomous decisionmakers.

III.1. *The Shoemaker–Farmer Model*

In order to study an "incapsulating" process in the exchange system, Frisch constructed a couple of simple two-sector models. (Only the simplest one is discussed here.)

---

[1] In fact, its content was more reminiscent of Henryk Grossmann (1929) than Kalecki, if we compare with Marxian economists. There was, however, no trace of Frisch being influenced directly by the Marxian authors who stressed the falling rate of profit as the dominant cause, although he might have been influenced by Marx himself.

Frisch began by assuming only two groups of persons called "shoemakers" and "farmers". They could only buy or sell their commodities at fixed points in time, "market days". Prices were assumed to be constant.

$X_{f,t}$ value of farm products sold by farmers on market day t.
$X_{s,t}$ value of shoes sold by shoemakers on market day t.
$C_{f,t}$ value of shoes bought by farmers on market day t.
$C_{s,t}$ value of farm products bought by shoemakers on market day t.

For both groups Frisch assumed that the value of what the group bought on one market day was proportional to what it had sold on the preceding market day:

$$C_{f,t} = \alpha X_{f,t-1} \qquad (1)$$

$$C_{s,t} = \beta X_{s,t-1} \qquad (2)$$

α and β are assumed to be positive constants. The value sold must be equal to the value bought for each commodity on every market day:

$$C_{f,t} = X_{s,t} \qquad (3)$$

$$C_{s,t} = X_{f,t} \qquad (4)$$

It is perhaps worth recalling that $X_{s,t}$ and $X_{f,t}$ was not assumed to be equal. Even if there were only two groups in this model, one group could sell for a greater value than the other did. With the exception of gifts, this situation is difficult to imagine without the creation of debt relationships or the transfer of cash. In this way a kind of monetary mechanism is presupposed.

The general solution of (1)–(4) with respect to $X_{f,t}$ is

$$X_{f,t} = K_1(\sqrt{\alpha\beta})^t + K_2(-\sqrt{\alpha\beta})^t \qquad (5)$$

K_1 and K_2 are constants determined by the initial situation. $\sqrt{\alpha\beta}$ determines the behavior of the system over time. If $\alpha<1$ and $\beta<1$, $\sqrt{\alpha\beta}<1$. (5) implies then that the sale of farm products is approaching zero. And so will the sales of shoes. But α and β less than one constitutes precisely the condition for saying that the sellers are in a "depressive" mood. To a certain extent we may say that the groups have been affected by a "saving panic".[1]

The model was also so simple that it bordered on banality. Still, it was

---

[1] It may be difficult to deal with saving in a model with equations such as (3) and (4). *Ex post* saving has to be zero. But if $\alpha<1$, $\beta<1$ both groups expect to sell more than they expect to buy. Total *ex ante* saving can thus be defined by:

$$S_t = (1-\alpha)X_{f,t-1} + (1-\beta)X_{s,t-1}$$

where S_t is equal to planned saving for market day t. Realized saving has to be zero. Thus, this model has something in common with Frisch's verbal utterances about the "saving panic", where he insisted on how attempts to save might drag down production and employment.

striking and pointed out the problem of effective demand. Compared to many of the modern theories of "disequilibrium" where static methods are used (see, for instance, Malinvaud (1977)), Frisch's derivation of the "perceived constraints" is more simple-minded, but possibly more easy to understand.

When the model is "measured" by how well it served Frisch's own intentions, I do not think it was quite successful. The model could not give any explanation of how the monetary system might release the mode of behavior studied in the model. This problem was better dealt with by Frisch in the latter part of "Circulation Planning" (1934).

There he examined the possibility of creating a center for multilateral bartering without using money and where such "incapsulating" phenomena were unthinkable. He thus used one of the oldest, but perhaps by now not so highly regarded, methods for clear thinking about social problems—the utopian.

III.2. *The National Exchange Organization*

In addition to the ordinary banking system, Frisch thought another and more active system of multilateral exchange, a National Exchange Organization, should be created. He conceived of this new system as organized along the following lines.

First, a center should be established, whose main task would be to make calculations and give and ask the members for the necessary information.

In order to faciliate the mathematical treatment, Frisch assumed that each member only delivered one homogeneous product or service. Frisch's main idea was now to let the calculation center begin by asking each member how much he would be willing to buy from each other member, on the assumption that he could sell his good for the same amount as his total buying. Prices were assumed constant.

After all these wishes, or preliminary orders, were registered, the center would collect them and treat them as data. As all members had expressed their wishes independently, it would be sheer luck if the total of what the other members were willing to buy of each good were equal to what the producer had said he was willing to supply. If not, the center would have to adjust the original wishes by some means in order to clear all markets. The originality of Frisch's approach in this respect was not only that he demonstrated that this problem could be solved; but also that he showed different ways of *how* this could be done.

Before the process started, the center had to inform the members about the principles of adjustment to be used.

The simplest principle of adjustment Frisch suggested[1] was that in order to

---
[1] Frisch also worked with other and more complicated principles of adjustment, which required that the center could solve non-linear programming problems. He worked out

clear the markets, the center could adjust all the total quantities originally supplied and demanded by each member, without changing their relative magnitudes. One reason for this was that Frisch assumed fixed coefficients in production. By introducing this principle of adjustment, he demonstrated that the total relative composition of demands (or supplies) in the new circulation system would be determined, but not the total level of production. He determined this by an "axiom of freedom": no member could be asked to supply a greater value than he had been willing to supply the first time he had stated his wishes to the center. This implied that the member who produced the good which was, relatively, the most scarce inside this exchange system determined the scale of turnover and production. The calculation problem was now solved.

Instead of giving each member orders for what he was supposed to supply, Frisch believed that the individuals would have a greater sense of freedom if they received commodity notes printed by the center.[1] In order to be insured against threats of saving, the notes could only be used within a fairly short period of time. The use of commodity notes made it possible to preserve something of the decentralized "matchings" of buyers and sellers performed by a monetary system.

"Circulation Planning" was a very special piece of work. Its economic content had deep roots in utopian thinking by trying to solve the old problems of overproduction and the difficulties of selling by means of a monetary scheme. (John Gray's *Social System* from 1831 was an early attempt at this kind of solution.) Frisch tried to solve the difficulties inherent in selling by this moneyless clearing system which was supposed to supplement the existing "old fashioned" banking system. He was, to my knowledge, the first in this tradition who seriously tried to solve the problems of market clearing.

While the existing banking sector was composed of different decision centers that often worked against each other and only passively affected the exchange transaction without giving the transactors any information about how much they could expect to sell, the new National Exchange Organization would make centralized decisions and give the members such information.

Though Frisch's analytical treatment of multilateral clearing was probably more inspired by Walras' theory for general economic equilibrium than by Wicksell's monetary theory, it also showed his concern about the functioning of the banks and of the existing monetary system during a depression. In this way his "Circulation Planning" might be considered a continuation of the ambitious programme of Wicksell's monetary economics aimed at clarifying

---

an iteration that could solve the problem. But the primary interest of Frisch's discussion of these points is in the history of theory of economic planning or in the history of the use of analytical techniques in economics. It has less interest in a study of Frisch's monetary theories and accordingly will not be treated here.

[1] A commodity note can only be used to buy the commodity for which it is issued. To discuss the advantages of using commodity notes and not orders, the assumption of only one seller of each good had to be relinquished. Frisch did this in his discussion of the more practical aspects of his scheme.

how different monetary systems made the other parts of the economy work differently.

Frisch's solution for the ancient difficulties of selling had many evident weaknesses. For one thing he dealt too easily with the role of prices[1] and other motivational factors. And if it was as easy to sell as to buy in Frisch's "Circulation Planning", as compared to the monetary system, this was partly due to the fact that it was more difficult to buy. As a peculiarity, it might be mentioned that the only time Frisch's ideas were put into real practice, the experiment had to be given up because the members of the exchange system were not willing to fill in the detailed list for desired quantities that was necessary in order for the center (Frisch's economic-statistics laboratory at the Institute of Economics, Oslo) to make the calculations required.

If the curious article "Circulation Planning" had old roots, it also had some modern features, and not only in its analytical methods. It was an early study of the "logistics" of money and non-money market systems which, as far as I can ascertain, have only recently began to be studied by Clower, Leijonhufvud, and Ostroy & Starr.

III.3. *The "Incapsulating" Process in the Banking Sector*

In a report to the Norwegian government (Frisch, 1935b) and elsewhere, Frisch stressed the money destruction caused by individual bankers during an economic depression, the "scrambling" for liquidity. In this report Frisch once again revealed his interest in the monetary system in explaining the causes of the economic crisis. However, it was not very closely related to Wicksell's research program for studying the interaction of the "real" and monetary sectors. In fact, it was probably primarily inspired by the now almost forgotten Italian economist, Marco Fanno (who in turn, however, was much influenced by Wicksell).

III.4. *"Saving Panic"*

Frisch probably regarded the "saving panic" as the most destructive process released during a crisis. Paradoxically, he never gave a scientific analysis of this phenomenon. The discussion of this subject presented in his published works from this period consisted only of some short verbal remarks. They were, by the way, clearly inspired by Wicksell's discussion of the consequences of people trying to save in a monetary system with cash but without banks (Wicksell, 1935, pp. 7–8).

It is possible, however, to learn something more about Frisch's views on

---

[1] When Frisch returned to some of the ideas from "Circulation Planning" after World War II, he gave the role of prices at least a summary treatment, and the center was now also expected to quote prices. But he then only considered the system used to regulate international trade. For domestic purposes, he probably regarded the complicated clearing system as unnecessary.

the relation between saving, investment and the role of the monetary system by studying his interpretation of Wicksell. Indeed, one important reason why Frisch never published anything in this field was probably that he regarded Wicksell's analysis on this point to be sufficient.

IV. Frisch's Studies on Wicksell's Monetary Theory

References to Wicksell are dispersed throughout Frisch's various macroeconomic works from the thirties, his popular writings, speeches and scientific works. In 1934 he gave a systematic exposition of his view on Wicksell's theory of the "cumulative process", mostly based on Wicksell's *Lectures II*.

IV.1. *Frisch's Wicksell-model from 1934*

In the Autumn of 1934, Frisch started a series of lectures about monetary theory in the form of criticisms and expositions of past and present economists. The first theory to be discussed was Wicksell's. Possibly hoping to make Wicksell's theory more accessible, Frisch depicted the main points by means of simple dynamic equation systems. In these lectures he tried to follow Wicksell closely. Like Wicksell's analysis, Frisch's was built around the entrepreneurs' or investors' investment decisions and savers' or capitalists' saving decisions; the passive or active behavior of the banks was also studied. The problem to be dealt with concerned the variations in the general price level.

Frisch's interpretation began by looking into the entrepreneur's use of capital, not the use of existing fixed capital, but "fluid capital". He did not think this kind of capital actually had any concrete shapes, but that it manifested itself only as a supply of saved money at a certain point in time.

Frisch's interpretation of Wicksell concerning the assumed relation between the productivity rate, the value of fluid capital and the rate of inflation was:

$$q = f\left(I, \frac{\dot{p}}{p}\right), \quad \frac{\partial f}{\partial \frac{\dot{p}}{p}} > 0, \quad \frac{\partial f}{\partial I} < 0, \tag{1}$$

where

I is the value of the flow of fluid capital that the entrepreneurs can dispose of at a given point in time, measured by the monetary unit

q is the "productivity rate" (Frisch defined the productivity rate as the marginal rate of profit the entrepreneurs can expect to gain by investing the last unit of fluid capital)

$\frac{\dot{p}}{p}$ is the rate of change in the general price level.

Since q was the nominal rate of return, it was reasonable to assume that an (expected) rise in the price level would mean an increase in the productivity rate. In assuming price-taking behavior (the entrepreneurs neither behaved as monopolists nor, perhaps more relevant, felt rationed regarding the amount of investment), the productivity rate had to be equal to the interest the investors were willing to pay for borrowing an amount equal to I, when the rate of price changes was $\dot{p}/p$. On the assumption of price-taking behavior, (1) might be interpreted as both a micro or a macro relation. The entrepreneurs could only borrow from the banks. For a given loan interest, i_u, the investors would adjust the amount of investment until:

$$i_u = q. \tag{2}$$

For the capitalists' saving behavior Frisch assumed:

$$i_T = G\left(S, \frac{\dot{p}}{p}\right) \quad \frac{\partial G}{\partial S} > 0 \quad \partial \frac{\partial G}{\partial \dot{p}/p} > 0 \tag{3}$$

where

S is the value of saving per time unit,
i_T is the interest the capitalists demand for lending.

The savers could only lend their money to the banks. He assumed that the capitalists did not feel rationed. (The banks could not refuse to receive deposits.) i_T then had to be equal to the interest on deposits. In order to simplify, he assumed the interest on deposits to be equal to the interest on loans:

$$i_u = i = i_T \tag{4) and (5}$$

where i was the common rate of interest.

(1)–(5) had seven variables and two degrees of freedom. Frisch now defined the normal rate of interest as the value of the rate of interest which satisfied (1)–(5) *and* the requirement that the value of saving was equal to the value of investment:

$$S = I \tag{6}$$

(1)–(6) now had one degree of freedom. The rate of change in the price level was assumed to be exogenously given. Frisch then obtained a relationship between the normal rate of interest and the rate of inflation:

$$n = H\left(\frac{\dot{p}}{p}\right). \tag{7}$$

where n is the normal rate of interest.

It can be shown that due to the signs of the derivatives assumed in (1) and (3), $\partial H/\partial(\dot{p}/p) > 0$. In the system (1)–(6) the equilibrium value of the saving and investment depend also on the rate of price change. Frisch gave the following reason for introducing the (expected) rate of price change:[1]

"Thus getting the normal rate of interest to change with certain changes in business conditions [$(\dot{p}/p)$ in this presentation of Frisch on Wicksell; my note] is an essential point in the theory. Suppose that we assumed the supply and demand to be independent of the changes in the price level ... The normal rate of interest would then be locked, and constant. But this concept of the natural rate of interest did not fit into Wicksell's reasoning. As we shall see later, Wicksell strongly emphasized the fluctuation in the normal rate of interest during an economic cycle. He even denoted these fluctuations as the 'essence of the so-called good and bad times'"[2] (my translation).

But did Wicksell believe that saving and investment were equal in the short run? The answer, according to Frisch, was no. In order to look at this question more closely, one had to study the behavior of the "go-between", the banks.

On the money market, the banks acted as auctioneers. They were large organizations dominated by routines, which also left their mark on the banks' interest-setting behavior. The banks were only expected to change their interest rates infrequently and accordingly, there were no reasons to expect that they would always set this rate equal to the normal rate. A more realistic picture of the working of the economy in short run is obtained if (6) is replaced by:

$$i = \underset{\cdot}{i}, \tag{6'}$$

where $\underset{\cdot}{i}$ denotes that the banks *set* the rate of interest autonomously. (Usually $\underset{\cdot}{i} \neq n$.) But what would then happen to the relation between the capitalists' saving and the entrepreneurs' investments? They would also have to differ.

If $\underset{\cdot}{i} > n$ and nothing immediately happened to the expected rate of price change, it follows from the signs of the derivatives that $I - S < 0$, and if $\underset{\cdot}{i} < n$, then $I - S > 0$. Frisch then supposed that the difference between the normal rate of interest and the market rate set by the banks could be used to describe the capitalists' and investors' reactions to changes in the market rate. He assumed:

---

[1] Wicksell is often accused of neglecting the effects of expected price changes. As we have seen, Frisch did not interpret him this way. Although it seems that Wicksell usually assumed that all changes in prices were unexpected by investors and savers, I do not think this part of Frisch's interpretation is in conflict with Wicksell's ideas. Wicksell primarily disregarded the expected rate of change in the price level because this factor only strengthened his conclusions; see Wicksell (1936), pp. 96–97.

[2] For his own part, and Frisch was now definitely moving away from Wicksell without being aware of it, Frisch stressed the possibility that the normal rate of interest might be negative during a strong deflation. This implied that the Wicksellian policy proposal for regulating the price level had to be impractical during strong deflation periods, given the existing monetary institutions. (It meant that one would be paid interest if one borrowed.)

$$\frac{I-S}{S} = u\left((i-n), \frac{\dot{p}}{p}\right), \frac{\partial u}{\partial (i-n)} < 0, ^1 \frac{\partial u}{\partial \left(\frac{\dot{p}}{p}\right)} > 0. \tag{8}$$

But what did $I-S \neq 0$ mean in a closed economy? Frisch apparently meant that $I-S \neq 0$ was possible both in an *ex ante* and an *ex post* sense. He attributed this to the special characteristics of the money market:

"A peculiarity of a money market (in contrast to a commodity market) is that supply and demand do not have to be equal, because any possible difference can be created or absorbed by the system itself, that is, by credit inflation or credit deflation, respectively. It is this point which makes the dynamics of the monetary system interesting. It was also exactly this point which Wicksell grasped and developed" (my translation; unpublished manuscript).

Even if the market rate differed from the normal rate, both savers and investors might have their plans realized by the banks passively fulfilling their demands and supplies.

In this exposition of Wicksell's theory, Frisch did not treat the problems related to the saving and investment concepts. But in a series of lectures in the Spring of 1935, Frisch (1935a) gave it an extensive treatment.[2] Here Frisch introduced the problem as follows:

"The discrepancy between saving and investment is the heart of Wicksell's theory. And in this theory the concepts of saving and investment are mostly used in the previously defined sense—which implies that they are quantities that may be different only in an *ex ante* sense. On the other hand, it is clear that Wicksell, in studying the consequences for the monetary system, was also dealing with a discrepancy which may be positive or negative *ex post*. There seems to be a contradiction here. Following Wicksell's thought to the end, however, the contradiction dissolves" (1935a, p. 34, my translation).

In order to conceive of a difference between saving and investment *ex post*, Frisch (1935a) started an almost axiomatic discussion:

"In order to arrive at a difference between saving and investment, the concepts obviously have to be tied to a *transaction* between two or more groups. And the transactions have to be treated in a special way. Among others, two conditions must be fulfilled (here). First, *a certain kind of value transfers* should be distinguished and should not be included in the saving-investment balance. Second, a certain group of persons or institutions should

---

[1] Frisch supposed that only the difference between the two concepts of interest rates was important for $(I-S)/S$. But with general functions in (1) and (3) this does not look convincing; also the levels of the interest variables should be arguments. Haavelmo (1944, pp. 33-38), however, has shown that only the difference counts if the functions are linear.

[2] In these lectures he intended to formulate a system of concepts and accounting relations in order to compare the monetary theories of Wicksell, Lindahl, Keynes, Ohlin, etc. It also was one of the building blocks in Frisch's work on national accounting in the late thirties.

be distinguished and their dispositions should not be included in the saving-investment balance" (p. 34; my translation).

More precisely, what Frisch had in mind was to treat the banks as one separate sector and to deal with the transfer of cash between banks and the public in a special way.

He ended this discussion by defining two new concepts: S_F as financial saving, which Frisch defined as equal to the sum of the net change in the public's stock of deposits and its net buying of securities and I_F as financial investment, which Frisch defined as equal to the net change in the stock of loans and net selling of securities. He then got:

$$S_F - I_F = -\dot{M},$$

where $\dot{M}$ was the change in the public's stock of cash. A realized, positive surplus of saving had to be accompanied by a drain of cash from the public to the banks.

This way of clarifying his definitions did not have great consequences for Frisch's interpretation of Wicksell, as he assumed that a positive *ex ante* difference between saving and investment would result in a positive difference between the corresponding *ex post* financial concepts. Frisch believed that this was the reason why Wicksell sometimes regarded "the saving discrepancy as a planned and sometimes as a realized magnitude, and perhaps at some times incompletely specified the difference" (p. 37; my translation).

Even after the World War II, Frisch was convinced about the fruitfulness of allowing saving to be different from investment *ex post*. In his article on Wicksell from 1951–52, he wrote:

When one has become aware that the problem must be handled from an ecosirk (*tableau économique*) viewpoint, the path of least mental resistance undoubtedly leads to saying that actual investment is by definition always equal to actual saving. I am convinced however that this is not the solution we need. I vividly remember the deception I felt one evening in Kings College many years ago when Keynes told me that he had finally decided to make actual investment equal to actual saving. I am sure that this was a step backwards in the *General Theory* as compared with his *Treatise on Money* (1951, p. 17).

As regards his interpretation of Wicksell from 1934, Frisch now only had to put the realized $(I_F - S_F)$ as a function of $I - S$ into (8) to interpret this as an equation of credit expansion or credit contraction.

But the system (1)–(6) still had one degree of freedom. What determined the variation in price level?

In order to explain this, Frisch—like Wicksell—began by conceiving of a situation where saving was equal to investment and total production was exogenously given. He then assumed the banks to lower the market rate of interest. The demand for investment would rise and at the same time intended saving would fall, or consumption demand would rise. As the total volume of production was given, this would imply total excess demand for goods, producers would raise their prices and the result would be a rise in the general price level.

$$\frac{\dot{p}}{p} = W(Z) \quad \frac{\partial W}{\partial Z} > 0 \quad W(0) = 0 \tag{9}$$

where $Z = (I - S)/S$. Frisch stressed the point that it was not the absolute levels of investment and saving that influenced the movement in the price level, but only the difference between them.

Frisch was still not satisfied with his Wicksell interpretation. Wicksell had believed that in the long run, the banks would move the market rate of interest in the direction of the normal rate, reacting to changes in their cash balance. (Implicitly, the assumption about a complete elastic credit system was thereby disregarded.) This might give an equation to replace (6') for determining the market rate as an endogenous variable. However, Frisch did not specify this relation analytically in his general Wicksell model, but only in a version with a linear specification of all relations.

Frisch's interpretation of Wicksell from 1934 was primarily inspired by the "positive solution" in Wicksell's *Lectures II*, and he did not refer to Wicksell's *Interest and Prices*. Accordingly, he interpreted Wicksell's saving and investment concepts as flow variables. The clearness of his exposition might be attributed to the fact that he was not worried about the relation between the cumulative process and Wicksell's theory of capital, perhaps at the cost of some superficiality[1] as compared with Lindahl and Myrdal. But his exposition was much clearer, especially his discussion of the relation between the normal and productivity rates. It is questionable whether Frisch came any closer to Wicksell's ideas.

On the paradigmatic level Frisch's interpretation revealed his fascination with the mode of behavior of the banks. It also stressed the disagreement between Wicksell and the ordinary quantity theory of money. An increase in the general price level was not caused by an increase in the public's cash

---

[1] In his interpretation after the War (1951 & 1952), Frisch also attempted to integrate these two parts of Wicksell's economics, this time based on *Interest and Prices*. In addition he discussed the more complicated institutional structure from this book with its four-group model (as compared with three in the *Lectures*), banks, entrepreneurs, capitalists and workers/landowners. But the building blocks in Frisch's 1934 interpretation was retained; the strict separation between the normal and productivity rate, where the normal rate was still an unobservable variable. He was still convinced about the fruitfulness of allowing the possibility of a difference between "saving" and "investment" *ex post*. But now "saving" and "investment" were stock variables, and discussing a stationary economy, the functions of interest rates were now to make the entrepreneurs willing to use and the capitalists willing to hold the existing stock of commodity capital. As the productivity rate was now related to the capital stock, and adjustments in stocks had to be time consuming, Frisch this time also discussed the possibility of a difference between the productivity rate and the market rate of interest, and not only between the market and the normal rate.

balance. The most important conditioning factor was the excess demand for goods that caused both an increase in the public's money stock as a consequence of the realized positive financial investment-saving difference, and made the entrepreneurs raise their prices. The changes in both the price level and the money stock were consequences of the same economic process. The relation between the money stock and the level of prices was a "coflux" relation, a relation with a lower degree of autonomy than the saving-investment functions.

IV.2. *Frisch's Views on Gunnar Myrdal's Interpretation of Wicksell*

Gunnar Myrdal developed his analysis of problems in monetary theory primarily as a critique of Wicksell (1931, 1933 & 1939). Frisch discussed Myrdal's interpretation in his 1934–35 lectures. He was very sceptical, and believed Myrdal had completely failed to understand Wicksell on some central points:

"We will formulate here our main point of view regarding our critical discussion of Myrdal's monetary theory. First, Wicksell's theory did not need any comprehensive revision as Myrdal has started. The only thing needed is a clear understanding of the three concepts θ, $\bar{\partial}$ and ∂ [i.e. the productivity rate, the normal rate and the market rate of interest, respectively; my note] as Wicksell obviously had in his mind.

Second, Myrdal's revision of Wicksell's theory is in Frisch's[1] opinion not in the spirit of Wicksell. It introduces new elements and most of the time it does not penetrate as deeply as Wicksell did" (my translation).

After these devastating remarks Frisch hastened to add that he found much that was valuable in Myrdal's work.

Frisch had two concrete criticisms to make. First, Myrdal had not understood the normal rate as formulated by Wicksell and confused it with the productivity rate. Second, Myrdal had not understood that the productivity rate expressed a marginal yield, and not an average yield, which Frisch thought to be a less relevant concept. (The same criticisms have been raised by Shackle (1967, p. 114) in an otherwise extremely positive evaluation of Myrdal's work in monetary theory.)

IV.3. *The 1934 Interpretation and its Consequences for Frisch's Own Views on the Relationship between Saving and Investment*

As mentioned, Frisch did not present any analysis of the saving-investment relationship. But some hints may be derived from his comments on Wicksell. In his 1934 model, Frisch tried to give a realistic picture of Wicksell's views, and in this interpretation he more or less retained Wicksell's assumption of a given level of total production. But as soon as he stopped reading Wicksell, he forgot this and ascribed to Wicksell his own view that the saving-investment

---

[1] As these were lecture notes, Frisch is mentioned in the third person. Frisch looked through these lecture notes thoroughly.

difference also caused quantity adjustments and changes in the total level of employment and production.

In a speech broadcast in 1932, Frisch (1932a) had concentrated on the consequences of price changes on the expected level of profit and on how the profit level affected the total level of production. He thus described Wicksell's theory of the cumulative process during a deflation:

"While the rate of profit during the upswing was less than it had to be if it were to be kept on a natural level, the situation during the downturn was reversed. Now the entrepreneurs had to buy the means of production while prices were high and sell their products when prices were lower. They then did not get enough profit to pay the interest on embodied capital and consequently, a continuous contraction of production follows" (1932a, pp. 127–128; my translation).

In his lectures about the conceptual scheme for comparing the different monetary theories (1935a), Frisch not only stressed the consequences of changes in prices on the activity level, but left open the question as to how the contraction got started. After explaining that a positive realized saving-investment difference implied a cash drain from the public, he continued:

"Wicksell's idea about the connection between the activity level, real capital and the monetary stock is clear: A positive *ex ante* saving difference means deflationary attitudes among the public (and eventually the state). It causes a positive *realized* financial saving difference—and thereby a decline in the monetary stock of the public (and eventually the state), to falling prices and contraction on the activity level" (1935a, p. 37; my translation).

In the simple Keynesian models, a positive *ex ante* positive difference between saving and investment becomes "closed" by a decline in the net national product and a new equilibrium level is established. The quantity of money is constant. Frisch, however, probably believed that a cumulative process of contraction might keep the saving gap open.[1] This was surely not the Wicksellian theory of the cumulative process.

From a historical point of view it is thus interesting to note how easily an active social scientist such as Frisch, buried in the problems of his own times, ascribed to his admired predecessor Wicksell, his, Frisch's, own views. On the other hand, these partly false perceptions of Wicksell were the most fruitful in developing Frisch's own ideas.

V. Wicksell's Influence on Frisch and a Comparison between Them

Normally it might be difficult to trace an influence from one economist to another and the results might be based mostly on guesswork. I do not believe

---
[1] In order to explain this Frisch either had to assume a kind of acceleration principle to drive the investment down, or he had to assume that the cash drain pushed down consumption and/or investment demand. Regarding his other writings (1931–32 & 1933), Frisch would probably stress both the effect of the money stock on consumption demand and the acceleration effects on the investment from the decline in consumption.

this to be the case here. Frisch often drew attention to the fact that he regarded Wicksell as his most important teacher in what is today called macroeconomics. It has also been shown that Frisch devoted a great deal of work to studying Wicksell's monetary theory. But as soon as we ask what this influence consisted of in more precise terms, it immediately becomes more difficult to answer. Strictly speaking, they had chosen rather different fields of research. While Frisch, as most of the other outstanding economists in the thirties, was primarily interested in explaining movements in capacity utilization and unemployment, Wicksell's interest had been focused on the movement in prices. In his analytical works, Wicksell had not written much about crisis, and I think his discussion of the matter revealed at great deal of confidence in the ability of the system of free competition to keep the unemployment level down.

All the same, Frisch—like his Swedish contemporaries—*did* go back to Wicksell in order to explain the economic depression. What did Frisch discover in Wicksell?

First of all, he found some ideas on important methodological matters. Wicksell's picture of the "rocking horse" which entered into regular fluctuations even if its movement was sustained by means of irregular pushes, made a great impression on Frisch. This idea directly inspired Frisch's work on the behavior of macrodynamic models when exposed to random shocks. Frisch also believed that Wicksell's use of the normal rate as a methodological device for studying the properties of the dynamic model might be useful, and Frisch accordingly tried to formulate a general methodological principle on this (Frisch, 1936). On a more general level, Frisch regarded Wicksell's theory about the cumulative process as a methodological ideal for constructing macroeconomic models: dynamic, determinate and mathematical in content without the usual "fogginess" that troubled monetary economics. And most important of all, Frisch evidently learned the importance of theory in economic research from Wicksell.

With respect to economic content, Frisch also received inspiration from Wicksell's monetary theory. Most important, perhaps, were some general attitudes of Wicksell which Frisch shared, especially Wicksell's insistence on the difficulties of moving from micro to macro and an awareness of the possibility of making false conclusions by using simple analogy deductions. These difficulties were mostly caused by the economic fact that, contrary to the Marshallian picture, the economic actions of individuals in a planless economy often undermined the intended consequences of the others' actions, thus making it misleading to jump from the plan of an individual to the total result. A macroeconomic theory had to be constructed. Wicksell's analysis of the role of money as a store of value in an economy with cash but without banks directly influenced Frisch's own view on the role of saving.

Frisch regarded as fascinating Wicksell's theories about the actions of and reactions from the banking system to other parts of the economy and his way of "lifting up" the study of these half-mystifying subjects to a theoretical level. This evaluation of Frisch revealed itself in may ways.

First, in his popular writings, Frisch clearly "blamed" the behavior of the banking system for much of the responsibility regarding the development of the crisis, in much the same way that Wicksell pointed out the sluggish adjustments of interest rates on the part of the banks as the decisive reason why unfortunate inflation or deflation processes may cumulate.

Second, in his important article "Circulation Planning", Frisch analyzed a system of multilateral exchange, but without any common means of payment or any stores of value, and no possibility of economic contractions. By means of a detour, Frisch analyzed the problems of establishing a system of signals within a monetary economy which might guide the system out of unemployment situations. After a while, as the depression continued, Frisch's attitudes toward the bankers grew into an almost aggressive hostility, and he began talking about the "ignorant monetary plutocracy", and so on.

Third, Frisch's concern for the banks was expressed in his early work on national accounting and in his disappointment with Keynes' definition of saving and investment in *General Theory* that made it difficult to disclose the role of the banks in saving and investment processes.

And fourth, this interest also appeared in his methodological studies, such as his well-known "Propagation Problems and Impulse Problems" (1933*a*, pp. 9–10) where it was the "monetary brake" that was "responsible" for the contractions.

But Frisch never did come to construct a detailed macroeconomic theory of a capitalist economy with a specified banking sector. This part of his work remained unfinished, giving flashes of insight, but never really competing with e.g. Keynes' attempts to construct a systematic macroeconomic theory. As his interest in monetary theory, contrary to Wicksell's, according to Gårdlund (1958, pp. 273–275) was primarily practically motivated, he was less interested in monetary economics after the beginning of the Second World War. He then concentrated on national accounting and methodological works, and after the War Frisch became especially interested in the economics of planning.

His interest in Wicksell, however, was more extensive than could be deduced from the problems Frisch was concerned with. We have seen how he put a great deal of work into his interpretations of Wicksell. If one asks why Frisch became occupied with Wicksell's theories in the thirties, I would answer that in addition to the purely great intellectual qualities he found in Wicksell, there was something common to their views of society that was predisposing. Both might be said to belong to the radical part of the *bourgeoisie*, both were preoccupied by problems they believed *everybody* had to be interested in solving (inflation and unemployment, respectively), problems created by almost invisible and anonymous forces within the circulation system, that among other things caused unnecessary strife between the different economic classes. Or to quote from an interview with Frisch from a much later date, where he talked about a Chinese dancing ensemble visiting Oslo, he said he found it: "... fantastically illustrating for my way of posing economic problems. The dance portrayed a fight performed in complete darkness. Then the light broke through and it became apparent that friends had fought bitterly, because they had not seen each other, just as different groups in our economic life are doing. Had they seen each other clearly, they would have understood immediately that cooperation based on rational economic compromises would have given everybody greater material happiness" (*Dagbladet*, 18-10-1958; my translation).

The "ignorant monetary plutocracy" was mainly responsible for the "darkness".

Even if there were many similarities between Wicksell's and Frisch's "visions" of the economy, of course, there was a lot of disagreement, too. Most important, I think, was that while Wicksell viewed the economy as dominated by a scarcity which no institutional change could really relieve in the short run, and only a fall in the rate of population growth could improve in the longer run, Frisch viewed an economy with considerable unused productive forces, unused primarily because of faults in the way the economy was organized. Consequently he thought it possible to make great economic improvements also in the short run.

References

Unpublished

Archive boxes nos. 5, 34, 35, 41 and 92 from the archives of Ragnar Frisch at the Institute of Economics, University of Oslo.

Archive boxes nos. 1, 2, 3 of the letter archive of Frisch's scientific correspondence at the Manuscript Department of the Royal University Library, Oslo.

Published

Frisch, Ragnar: Konjunkturbevegelsen som statistisk og økonomisk fenomen. In *Förhandlingar ved Nordiska Nationalekonomiska møtet i Stockholm, 15–17 juni 1931*. 1931a.

Frisch, Ragnar: Johan Åkerman: Om det ekonomiska livets rytmikk. *Statsvetenskaplig Tidsskrift*, 1931b, pp. 281–300.

Frisch, Ragnar: Konjunkturene. In *Verdensøkonomien i efterkrigstiden* by Wilhelm Keilhau, Ingvar Wedervang &

Ragnar Frisch, Universitetets radioforedrag, Serie B, Nr. 6. Oslo 1932a.

Frisch, Ragnar: Statens plikt til cirkulasjonsregulering (hastily jotted down, 10–12 December 1932); published as *Memorandum fra Sosialøkonomisk institutt*, Universitetet i Oslo, Oslo, 11. januar 1951). 1932b.

Frisch, Ragnar: Propagation problems and impulse problems in dynamic economics. In *Economic Essays in Honor of Gustav Cassel*. London, 1933, pp. 171–205.

Frisch, Ragnar: *Sparing og cirkulasjonsregulering*. Oslo, 1933b.

Frisch, Ragnar: *Forelesninger holdt 1933^{II} og 1934^{I} over Makrodynamikk*. Oslo, 1934a.

Frisch, Ragnar: Circulation Planning. *Econometrica*, pp. 258–336 and pp. 422–435, 1934b.

Frisch, Ragnar: Et generelt monetært begrep og symbolsystem. In *Professor*

Frisch's forelesninger over Moderne Pengeteorier. Vårsem. og høstsem. 1935. Oslo, 1935a.

Frisch, Ragnar: 'Open Market Operations' og deres virkninger på banksystemet. Bilag 4 til Innstilling om markedsoperasjoner. Komiteen til utredning av økonomiske og pengepolitiske spørsmål, Oslo, 1935b.

Frisch, Ragnar: On the notion of equilibrium and disequilibrium. Review of Economic Studies, pp. 100–105, 1936.

Frisch, Ragnar: Noen trekk av konjunkturlæren. Oslo, 1947.

Frisch, Ragnar: Frisch on Wicksell. In The development of economic thought (ed. H. W. Spigel), New York, 1952. Also printed as a Memorandum fra Sosialøkonomisk institutt, Universitetet i Oslo, 15. desember 1951 entitled Knut Wicksell, A cornerstone in modern economic theory. 1951.

Gray, John: The social system (Reprint, New Jersey, 1973). 1831.

Gårdlund, T.: The life of Knut Wicksell. Stockholm, 1958.

Haavelmo, T.: The probability approach in econometrics. Econometrica, vol. 12, Supplement, 1944.

Landgren, K.-G.: Den nya ekonomien i Sverige. J. M. Keynes, E. Wigforss, B. Ohlin och utvecklingen 1927–39. Uppsala, 1960.

Malinvaud, Edmond: The theory of unemployment reconsidered. Oxford, 1977.

Myrdal, Gunnar: Monetary equilibrium (Reprint, N.Y., 1965). 1939.

Myrdal, Gunnar: Om penningteoretisk jämvikt. Ekonomisk Tidskrift, 1931.

Myrdal, Gunnar: Der Gleichgewichtsbegriff als Instrument der geldtheoretischen Analyse. Wien, 1933.

Ostroy, J. M. & Starr, Ross M.: Money and the decentralization of exchange. Econometrica, 1974, pp. 1093–1113.

Samuelson, Paul M.: Foundation of economic analysis. (Reprint, Cambridge Mass., 1965.) 1947.

Shackle, G. L. S.: The years of high theory. Cambridge, 1967.

Steiger, Otto: Studien zur Entstehung der Neuen Wirtschaftslehre in Schweden. Berlin, 1971.

Wicksell, Knut: Interest and prices. London, 1936.

Wicksell, Knut: Lectures on political economy. Volume II: Money (Reprint, 1967). 1935.

WICKSELL, BOWLEY, SCHUMPETER AND THE DOLLS' EYES

Ingolf Ståhl

Stockholm School of Economics, Stockholm, Sweden

Abstract

This article aims at drawing attention to Wicksell's last important contribution to economic theory, namely his model for bilateral monopoly.[1] This aspect of Wicksell's work has not received its proper attention, mainly because the model that should have been called the Wicksell model is known in the literature as the Bowley model. For half a century this model—implying a determinate solution of the bilateral monopoly problem—has competed with models implying that this problem is indeterminable on economic grounds, at least as regards price. The most recent research in this area, however, has given at least partial support to the Wicksellian idea that bilateral monopoly has a determinate solution, in that a completely determinate solution can be established on the basis of economic factors alone for many situations.

I. Statement of the Problem

Our article deals with Wicksell's last important contribution in the field of theoretical economics, namely his review of Bowley's book *Mathematical Economics*, published in *Ekonomisk Tidskrift* in 1925, where he established a determinate model of bilateral monopoly.

We begin with the picturesque examplification given by Wicksell, who in turn had borrowed it from Babbage,[2] namely the following:

An English toy manufacturer, who had hitherto had to import dolls' eyes, was eventually successful after a long search in London in finding a consumptive Italian glass blower, who understood the art of producing dolls' eyes and with his help he established a flourishing trade in this article.

---

[1] It can possibly be argued that Wicksell's article "Valutasporsmålet i de skandinaviska länderna" (The Currency Problem in the Scandinavian Countries) *Ekonomisk Tidskrift* 27, 1925, pp. 205–22 was later. Schumpeter's statement regarding the article studied as Wicksell's last contribution ("Indem das Archiv seinen Lesern die letzte Arbeit Knut Wicksells vorlegt") can, however, be accepted e.g. by regarding the *Valutasporsmålet* either as written earlier or as being of considerably less importance as regards economic theory. Similar arguments also appear to apply to Wicksell's article "Zur Zinstheorie (Böhm-Bawerks dritter Grund)", published posthumously in 1928.

[2] According to Machlup-Taber (1960).

We assume here a *buyer*, who is the only one interested in (or capable of) buying a specific good (e.g. dolls eyes), and a *seller*, who is the only one capable of furnishing these goods (e.g. the glass blower). Many situations in reality approximate this bilateral monopoly situation. This is e.g. the case of a manufacturer selling a specialized product on a foreign market through an agent who, for various reasons, is the only one competent or legally able to handle the sales of the products.[1] An important area for bilateral monopoly is also company-union bargaining in a place completely dominated by one industry and with all workers belonging to the same union.

We assume that the buyer of the goods in question in his turn resells the goods (possibly after some value-adding transformations) on a market, where quantity is a downward sloping function q of the market price p. He also has his own selling and transformation costs $C_B(q)$ and his total profit is written as $\pi_B = qp - C_B(q) - qP$, where P is the price that the buyer pays to the seller for each unit of the intermediate article. We study a time period long enough for equating final sales on the market with purchases of the intermediate product.

The seller's profit from this operation, π_S, can be written as $qP - C_S(q)$, where $C_S(q)$ denotes the seller's production costs varying with q.

We realize that the seller wants, *ceteris paribus*, as high a value as possible of P, while the buyer wants as low a value as possible.

The problem now is whether, on the basis of assumptions commonly used in economic theory, we can find a solution determining (1) what quantity q and (2) what price P will be established.

II. Bilateral Monopoly Theory Prior to Wicksell

As stressed by Schumpeter no important economist prior to Wicksell had answered this question affirmatively.[2] A review of the literature substantiates this statement.

The first to discuss bilateral monopoly is Menger (1871).[3] In dealing with the case of "isolated exchange" Menger regarded "price" (i.e. the exchange

---

[1] In this connection we note a not uncommon practice among some agents on smaller markets. When they see a promising product coming up on some large market they register the trade name of this product in their own name on the small market, before the manufacturer has realized the benefit of taking this step on his own. Thus a genuine bilateral monopoly situation has arisen; see Ståhl (1967).

[2] Schumpeter (1927) writes the following about bilateral monopoly theory prior to Wicksell "... mit seltener Einhelligkeit haben alle Theoretiker von Namen ausdrücklich oder tatsächlich denselben Standpunkt [that P is indeterminate]". Schumpeter continues "Das ist um so merkwürdiger als er [Wicksell] einen Fall behandelt (den mit den Puppenaugen), der doch hierher gehört und in dem ihm selbst die Ableitung eines theoretisch bestimmten Gleichgewichtzustandes gelingt".

[3] It could be mentioned here that Schumpeter (1954) finds a Cesare Bonesano Marchese di Beccaria (1764) anticipating Menger in showing the indeterminateness of the exchange; see Machlup & Taber (1960).

conditions) to be indeterminate within certain limits. In this connection it should be stressed that Cournot does *not* deal with bilateral monopoly.[1]

The first somewhat rigorous analysis of bilateral monopoly goes back to Edgeworth (1881), who concludes that determination of price remains indeterminate, but the quantity is established by the contract curve, where a party can only be better off by making the other party worse off. A similar analysis is provided by Pareto (1896). The quantity in bilateral monopoly is established as that which maximizes the total joint profit, fulfilling the conditions of Pareto optimality.

This Pareto-optimal quantity q^0 is thus obtained when $\pi_B + \pi_S = qp - C_B(q) - qP + qP - C_S(q) = qp - C_B(q) - C_S(q)$ is maximized. For the linear case (i.e. with sloping demand curve $p = a - bq$ and $AC = MC$ (c_S and c_B) for both parties) this is obtained when $q(a - bq) - q(c_S + c_B)$ is maximized, i.e. when $a - 2bq = c_S + c_B$, that is $q^0 = (a - c_S - c_B)/2b$.

Prior to the article by Wicksell the theory of bilateral monopoly could hence be divided into two groups:

(1) Both quantity and price are indeterminate
(2) Quantity is determinate, but price is indeterminate.

The only indications of a determinate solution appear to be those given by Böhm-Bawerk (1889) and Pigou (1908), who indicate that price will most likely reflect some 50–50 divison. These hypotheses, however, are not based on economic theory assumptions, but rather on some vague notions of equal bargaining strength.

It is important to note that the authors arguing for a *determinate* quantity, do not indicate the *process* by which such a Pareto-optimal agreement is *reached* or the institutional assumptions regarding the form of bidding. The main argument is that an agreement outside of the Pareto-optimal contract curve of maximum joint profit cannot be stable, since *both* parties can increase their profits by moving to this curve.

The authors regarding also *quantity* as indeterminate focus on the procedure by which an agreement is reached. Very typical for this school is the passage

---

[1] Cournot (1838) discusses only the case of complementary monopolies which cannot, as erroneously claimed by e.g. Zeuthen (1930), be regarded as identical to the situation of bilateral monopoly. Although every complementary monopoly case (with two parties) can be turned into a bilateral monopoly situation by letting one of the monopolists become the purchaser of the other monopolists's products, very few bilateral monopoly situations can be turned into a complementary monopoly situation in a meaningful way, since the product or service of one party cannot meaningfully be provided separately from the other party's commodities. A labor union selling labor to e.g. a car manufacturer, cannot meaningfully sell its service directly to the public. It should in this connection also be stressed that the Cournot model, even when applied to those few bilateral monopoly situations which could meaningfully be turned into a complementary monopoly situation, will *not*, as sometimes erroneously claimed (see e.g. Ståhl (1965)), lead to the same solution as the Wicksell model. The main idea of the Cournot model is a simultaneous solution of an equation system and is hence more similar to the marginal intersection model.

in Bowley (1924) which in fact initiated Wicksell's article. We can quote him, using our notations, as writing:

> The manufacturer [= buyer] fixes in a particular P and produces q' to make his maximum. At the same P the labourer [= seller] furnishes q''. There may be a value of P for which $q' = q''$ but without collusion it will not be obtained.
>
> This result, that with one factor and one user of that factor the equations become indeterminate, is obtainable with less simple hypotheses; but the method used can be extended to show that universal monopoly of all factors and all production leads to indeterminate results.

III. The Wicksell Model

We have then reached the year of Wicksell's critique of Bowley. Wicksell cannot see the logic of the Bowley model and presents instead the following model, which is based on our, not Wicksell's, notations.[1]

The main reason why a determinate solution for both q and p is reached in the Wicksell model is that the seller can dictate the price, while the buyer alone determines quantity. It should be stressed that the model relies on both parties having complete information about demand and each other's costs.

The seller hence quotes a price P, and the buyer will next determine that q which maximizes $\pi_B(q, P)$. We hence obtain the optimal value of q as a function $q(P)$ by the equation $d\pi_B(q, P)/dq = 0$.

The seller then knows from $q(P)$ the quantity that will result from each possible value of P. Next he determines the optimal value of P by setting $d\pi_S(q(P), P)/dP = 0$. We thus obtain the determinate value of P, P^w, which inserted into the function $q(P)$ determines the solution value of q, q^w.

For our pay-off function $\pi_B = qp - qP - C_B(q)$, we obtain
$p + q \cdot p' - C'_B(q) - P = 0$ for determining $q(P)$.[2]

Next with $\pi_S = q(P)P - C_S(q(P))$ we determine P by

$$q(P) + \frac{dq(P)}{dP} P = \frac{dC_S(q)}{dq} \frac{dq(P)}{dP}.$$

For the case of a linear demand and constant marginal costs we hence determine $q(P)$ from $a - 2bq - c_B - P = 0$ i.e. $q = (a - P - c_B)/2b$.

Inserted into π_S we obtain $\pi_S = ((a - P - c_B)/2b)(P - c_S)$. We can obviously

---

[1] Wicksell uses, obviously for pedagogical reasons, knowing that the readers of *Ekonomisk Tidskrift* in 1925 knew hardly any mathematics, a linear demand curve of the simplest type, namely $q = 1 - p$, and sets $C_B = C_S = 0$. Thanks to this he even avoids using differentiation. These simplifications do not change the main behavioral idea of the solution concept.

[2] It should be mentioned that the second degree condition requires that $d(p + q \cdot p' - C'_B(q) - P)/dq < 0$, i.e. that $2p' + qp'' < C''_B(q)$, which with $p' < 0$, clearly holds if $p'' \leq 0$ and $C''_B(q) \geq 0$.

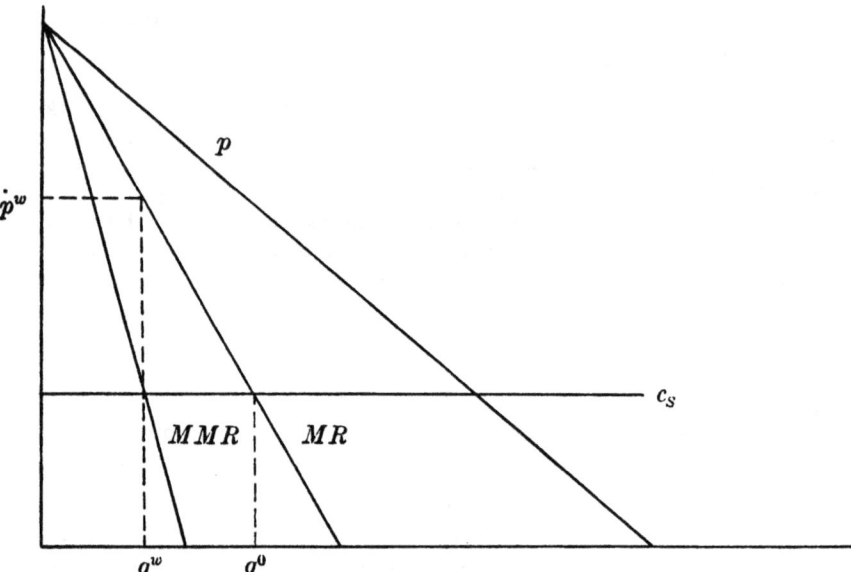

Fig. 1

disregard $1/2b$, maximize $(a-c_B)P-P^2+Pc_S$ and look for $a-c_B+c_S-2P=0$, i.e. $P^w=(a-c_B+c_S)/2$.

Hence $q^w = \dfrac{a-(a-c_B+c_S)/2-c_B}{2b} = \dfrac{a-c_B-c_S}{4b}$.

For this linear case the total joint profit is maximized at $q=(a-c_B-c_S)/2b$, i.e. the Wicksell quantity q^w is only half of the Pareto-optimal quantity, q^0.

The Wicksell model can be illustrated in this linear case by the simple figure above, in which we assume that $c_B=0$.

The Pareto-optimal quantity q^0 is obtained by $MR=MC(=c_S)$. In the Wicksell case the buyer, for each possible P, will set $MR=P$ and hence the MR-curve constitutes the *derived* demand curve $q(P)$. The seller then maximizes his profit by setting the marginal curve of this marginal revenue curve equal to $MC=c_S$.

IV. Bowley's Models, Inspired by Wicksell

The Wicksell model, first published in *Ekonomisk Tidskrift* (the predecessor of *The Scandinavian Journal of Economics*), received more general attention through Schumpeter, who had the article published after Wicksell's death in *Archiv für Sozialwissenschaften*, 1927, where he also wrote an introduction to the article, bringing special attention to Wicksell's model of bilateral monopoly. Schumpeter indicates here that earlier, he had been convinced about the indeterminateness of bilateral monopoly, but now, after having seen Wicksell's model, he accepts the idea that under certain conditions a determinate solution can be found.

The publication in the *Archiv* obviously brought the article to Bowley's attention and this inspired him to write his well-known article published in the *Economic Journal* in 1928. He presents here three different models; the *first* is that of Wicksell, although in a somewhat more generalized, although less pedagogical, form (but still using only linear demand functions).[1]

In its behavioral and institutional assumptions, the *second* model is very similar to that of the Wicksell model. But here it is the buyer who dictates P and the seller who determines q.

Thus we look first at the sellers maximum problem setting $d\pi_S/dq = 0$, i.e. $P = C'_S(q)$. In contrast to the Wicksell model,[2] the second-order conditions are troublesome. We require that $d(P - C'_S(q))/dq < 0$, i.e. that $C''_S(q) > 0$.

Hence the very probable case of $C''_S(q) = 0$, i.e. of $MC = AC$, cannot be analyzed. Besides the idea of the buyer dictating the price as appearing more unnatural, this limitation of the cost function has probably contributed to the fact that this second model has received very little attention in the literature.

The *third* model is the model which later came to be known as the "marginal intersection model", later proposed also by e.g. Boulding (1950) and Fouraker (1957). In this model both the seller and the buyer regard P as given, and for each P they will maximize their profit with regard to q.

The only possible solution is now that obtained when these $q(P)$-curves intersect, i.e. the solution is given by the simulatenous solution of the following system of equations: (1) $d\pi_B/dq = 0$; (2) $d\pi_S/dq = 0$.

The solution will obviously be Pareto-optimal, with $q = q^0$, since the equations above imply that $d\pi_B/dq + d\pi_S/dq = 0$, i.e. that $d(\pi_B + \pi_S)/dq = 0$.

This model, however, has the same flaw as model 2, limited in use to the case where $C''_S(q) > 0$. Furthermore, as already noted by Bowley, if $C''_S(q)$ is very small, i.e. if $C'_S(q)$ is an almost horizontal line, that is we almost have $AC = MC$, such as e.g. in the case where $C'_S(q) = c_S + q\varepsilon$, where ε is very small, then the seller will obtain a very small profit.

There are also other, more fundamental flaws. One can wonder why both parties should regard P as given. Either very specific institutional assumptions of some kind of market process are required to explain this, or the behavioral assumptions involve erroneous expectations. If e.g. the seller knew that the buyer assumes that P is given, then he himself would not assume that P is given. (Another flaw is discussed in Section VIII (c) below.)

---

[1] It should be stressed that Bowley mentions Wicksell's article, but the extent to which model 1 is Wicksell's is not seen very clearly from his article. If Bowley had called case 1 the Wicksell model, it is not unlikely that subsequent theory had used the more appropriate term Wicksell model instead of Bowley model.
[2] See footnote 2 on p. 171.

V. Critique against the Wicksell Model

The Wicksell model, known in theory as the Bowley model—see e.g. Hicks (1935), Tintner (1939), Fouraker (1957) and Siegel & Fouraker (1960)—received wide attention and was included in popular text books such as those of Allen (1937) and Schneider (1952).

For some time this Wicksell model and the Pareto-optimal model seemed to wage a fairly even struggle in theory. However, a certain uneasiness was noted in many cases regarding the fact that the Wicksell model leads to a non-Pareto-optimal outcome. As noted earlier both parties *could* obtain more after leaving the Wicksell solution, once having reached an agreement there. The unanswered question remained, however: by what procedure would they then reach a Pareto-optimal contract? The main problem was no doubt that all models indicating a Pareto-optimal solution, (except the marginal intersection model, generally not applicable), left P undertermined.

The discussion to some extent centered on the realism of the *institutional* assumptions required to obtain the Wicksell solution, in particular that one party stated price and the other determined quantity. In particular, Fellner (1947) stressed the importance of bargaining concerning *both* price *and* quantity simultaneously.

VI. Experimental Tests of the Wicksell Model

In an attempt to "settle the dispute between the Wicksell model and the Pareto model" laboratory experiments were then used. The first to conduct these were Siegel and Fouraker,[1] who tested the models for various institutional assumptions.

When the parties were allowed to quote both P and q, the evidence is overwhelmingly *against* the Wicksell model and *for* the Pareto solution (but in no way the marginal intersection solution), both for the case when both parties have complete and when they have incomplete information.[2]

In experiments involving the seller quoting P and the buyer quoting q, the evidence depends on the number of rounds involved as well as the information available. The more rounds and the more information, the more the outcome tended toward the Pareto-optimal quantity. This has to do with the fact that with many rounds available the buyer can afford to punish the seller for quoting too high a price by temporarily quoting a very low quantity.

Hence the experimental evidence for the Wicksell solution is not strong

---

[1] See Siegel & Fouraker (1960) and Fouraker & Siegel (1963). Among Swedish tests are those of Arvidsson (1973), Grubbström (1972) and Ståhl (1966).
[2] Incomplete information in the Siegel and Fouraker experiments implies that each party knows only his own profit. Ståhl (1966) tested an asymmetric information case, namely when the seller had complete, but the buyer incomplete information.

for situations characterized by what are probably the most common forms of bargaining. However, this does not necessarily rule out the Wicksell model as a model for rational bargainers in *all* situations.

VII. The Establishment of a Unique Value of P

The experimental results can very well be explained by search procedures unrelated to economic assumptions[1] and the Wicksell model retained its position in economic theory as long as the following question remained unanswered: how is a Pareto-optimal solution reached? Economic theory has been "paralyzed" in this respect as long as a determinate value of P cannot be assigned as a result of a process based on economic assumptions. Since 1930, beginning with Zeuthen, this has inspired many theories aimed at establishing a unique value of P.

This is not the place for a summary of all these theories.[2] It should only be stressed here that, as pointed out e.g. by Coddington (1973), all models presented prior to the seventies were lacking in at least one of the following two respects:

1. They were based on such extreme institutional assumptions that they could not become part of a more general theory;
2. They involved some kind of erroneous expectations as regards the opponent's behavior.

This was the background when I began my work on bargaining theory in the middle of the sixties. My starting point involved experimental tests of the Wicksell model. The particular experiment used included a stop rule. Analyzing the results, I began theorizing in a way very similar to dynamic programming. Then, in 1967, I succeeded in obtaining a unique solution for bargaining involving two alternatives (i.e. where P could take only one of two values) and in 1972, for n-alternative bargaining situations, i.e. where P could take one of any number of values.

It should be stressed that in contrast to other theories this theory only involves those behavioral assumptions commonly used in economic theory, e.g. profit maximizing firms that realize that the other party is also profit maximizing and finally that the parties have correct expectations about the other party's expectation (e.g. S knows that B knows that S is a profit maximizer, etc.).

In this article it should only be noted as regards this model that a unique value is obtained on the basis of an assumption that the parties' profits from a certain agreement decrease as an agreement is delayed, i.e. the model is dynamic

---
[1] Schenitzki (1962) hence obtains Pareto-optimal agreements in a model, where each bargainer bids a great many bids for each profit level, before lowering his profit request.
[2] This kind of survey is found in Coddington (1968) and Ståhl (1972).

in nature. Furthermore, a unique solution for P is obtained only for certain pay-off assumptions, e.g. the case when the pay-off from an agreement on a price P at time T can be written as $kP \int_T^Z e^{-rt} dt$, where k is a constant, Z is a point in time later than T and e^{-rt} is the discount factor. In other cases, most notably in the case of the pay-off function kPe^{-rT}, it can be proved that no unique solution can be obtained solely on the basis of the economic assumptions above.

Finally, it should be noted that for the case where P *is* determined, a Pareto-optimal solution value of q is obtained using the model. It should be stressed that we *first* establish that the *same* value of P is obtained for each value of q. It is then clear that rational bargainers will reach an agreement on the Pareto-optimal solution.

In all other cases, i.e. when P is *not* determined, it cannot be said that the "rational bargainers' solution" will be on the Pareto-optimal q^0, since it cannot be ruled out that one party believes he can obtain a "better" value of P at a $q \neq q^0$. Hence for those pay-off functions mentioned above, where a unique solution for P cannot be determined, the Wicksell solution cannot be ruled out.

VIII. Applications of the Wicksell Model

We now turn to three different aspects which point to the fact that the Wicksell solution can still be of relevance, or at least of greater relevance than most other early bargaining theories.

(a) Labor Management Bargaining

In the case of labor management bargaining one can discuss the extent to which bargaining concerns *both* P and q. Although in some countries (such as Sweden in recent years) unions have been given a greater say with respect to "hiring and firing", one can by and large state that in capitalist countries bargaining does not outright involve the total amount of production and employment, at least not at the same time.[1] Hence it is not unreasonable to assign a q-determining role to the buyer (management).[2] The question about the relevance of the Wicksell model then centers on whether the seller (the union) can dictate price, i.e. wages. Recent increases in union bargaining strength indicate that, at least in some branches in some countries, this might be a good approximation of reality. At the same time it should be stressed that in cases where very long strikes are not realistic alternatives, e.g. due to

---

[1] Negotiations about lay-offs, etc. usually take place at other times than wage negotiations. Furthermore, bargaining about lay-offs often takes place on a lower level than the most important wage negotiations.

[2] It should be stressed that here we deal with bargaining on a company or branch level, *not* on a national level, and that q is hence determined on microeconomic grounds.

government intervention, dynamic bargaining models such as mine lose their validity. Then the Wicksell model might in some instances be the best one available.

(b) The Buyer is Ignorant about the Seller's Costs

Another possible way the Wicksell solution can be used is as follows.[1] Let us assume that the buyer (e.g. an agent) has genuine uncertainty as to the seller's production costs, i.e. we leave our earlier assumption of complete information and go to the other extreme as regards one of the parties.

We here assume, for simplicity only,[2] that the buyer understands that the seller's production costs are characterized by constant AVC, i.e. constant $MC = c_S$. We furthermore assume that the seller in turn understands that the buyer lacks other information about the seller's costs. For the sake of simplicity we also assume that demand is linear, i.e. $p = a - bq$, that the seller's marginal costs are constant, i.e. $C_S(q) = qc_S$ and that C_B is negligibly small.

If the buyer is now ignorant about the seller's unit cost c_S, one can envisage a set of different solutions, determined by the Ståhl (1972) bargaining model with *one* solution for each *possible* value, c, of c_S. Each such solution $\{P(c), q^0(c)\}$ is characterized by $q^0(c)$ being the Pareto optimal quantity *if* the seller's costs actually were the "imagined" value c, i.e. $q^0(c) = (a-c)/2b$ (see p. 170). The "imagined" joint profit is then $q^0(a - bq^0 - c) = (a-c)^2/4b$ and P is then determined by $q^0(P - c) = x(a-c)^2/4b$, where x is the seller's share of the maximum joint profits. As noted, this share x is according to the mentioned bargaining model independent of the actual size of the maximum joint profits.[3] Hence

$$P - c = \frac{x(a-c)^2}{4b} \bigg/ \left(\frac{a-c}{2b}\right),$$

i.e. $P - c = x(a-c)/2$, i.e. $P = x(a-c)/2 + c$.

Thus, for a specific value of x, we can determine the set of possible agreement points, (P, q^0) depending on what value of c is contemplated.

We can next determine the profit that the seller would actually get if his real cost were c_S, although he was still successful in getting the buyer to believe that his cost was c. The seller will then, on top of the "open" profit $x(a-c)^2/4b$, also receive the "hidden profit" $q^0(c)(c - c_S)$, i.e. the actual value of π_S is then $(c - c_S)(a-c)/2b + x(a-c)^2/4b$.

Our question is: if the seller could fool the buyer into accepting any c as the true value, what is then the "optimal deception value" of c. In order to find this we maximize π_S as stated above with respect to c, i.e. (after multiplying by $4b$) we seek $\max_c 2(c - c_S)(a-c) + x(a-c)^2$. The first-order

---

[1] A similar idea was first discussed in Ståhl (1965).
[2] This assumption does not appear critical for the discussion.
[3] It is determined mainly on the basis of the parties' rate of time discount.

condition is then that $2(a-c)-2(c-c_S)-2x(a-c)=0$, implying that $a+c_S-ax=2c-cx$, i.e. that $c=(a+c_S-ax)/(2-x)$.

We note first that as the *limiting* case, when the seller has a very weak bargaining position, e.g. due to a very high discount rate in comparison to that of B, and hence x goes towards 0, we obtain that the "optimal deception value" goes towards $(a+c_S)/2$, which (with $c_B=0$) is equal to P^w, the Wicksellian exchange price.

The "imagined Pareto-optimal" quantity connected with $c=(a+c_S)/2$ is hence

$$\frac{a-(a+c_S)/2}{2b} = \frac{2a-a-c_S}{4b} = \frac{a-c_S}{4b};$$

which is q^w, the agreement quantity of the Wicksell model.

The Wicksell model is also of interest in this kind of situation when x is *not* close to zero, but any value <0.5 provided we assume:

(1) the buyer, in case of uncertainty, will use the maximin criterion and
(2) no side payments are possible.

For $x<0.5$, we can show that the Wicksell solution P^w, q^w will give the seller a *higher* profit than that which he could obtain by disclosing his true costs.[1]

Hence, if $x<0.5$ the seller would rather try to obtain the Wicksell solution than reveal his costs. The assumption above that the buyer acts according to the maximin criterion is then sufficient for deducing that the seller can enforce an agreement on P^w, if he, after earlier having only bid values $P>P^w$, claims that this variable unit cost $c_S=P_w+\varepsilon$. If this were true, no agreement could be reached on a $P<P_w$, since the seller would then not get any profits. The buyer would then have genuine uncertainty as to whether the seller speaks the truth or not. He can either accept P^w and with certainty obtain $q(p-P^w)$, which for $q<q^0$ is positive, or insist on a $P<P^w$ and then run a risk of obtaining 0. As a "maximiner" he will accept P^w.

It should finally be stressed that on the basis of our assumptions presented so far, we cannot deduce that the seller will really get exactly the Wicksell profit. We have only proved that he will *at least* get this much. If the buyer would openly assign a probability of 1 to the case of the seller always speaking the truth, then the seller would insist on c being the "optimal deception value", which would give the seller a higher profit than the one he will get from the Wicksell solution.[2]

---

[1] $\pi^S(P^w, q^w) = q^w(P^w-c_S) = \left(\dfrac{a-c_S}{4b}\right)\left(\dfrac{a+c_S}{2}-c_S\right) = (a-c_S)^2/8b$ while, with $x<1/2$, $\pi_S = x(\pi_S^0 + \pi_B^0) = x\left(\dfrac{a-c_S}{2b}\right)\left(a-\dfrac{a-c_S}{2}-c_S\right) < (a-c_S)^2/8b$.

[2] The Wicksell profit is then equal to the optimal profit only if $x=0$. Furthermore, the profit obtained from the "optimal deception value" increases with x since $d((c-c_S)(a-c)+x(a-c)^2)/dx = (a-c)^2 > 0$.

One cannot, however, say anything about the probabilities which B assigns to various values of c. The bargaining along the locus of unique bargaining outcomes for various values of c is determined according to completely different assumptions than those for determining the solution once c_S is given. While the latter case involves no risk or uncertainty, uncertainty is the main characteristic of the former situation. Hence it is in no way inconsistent to foresee the seller insisting on his costs c_S being close to P^w and that the buyer, although not assigning any high probability to $c=P^w$ and hence not accepting any agreement on P higher than P^w, will still be afraid of a complete break up and hence in a maximin spirit accept P^w.

The important thing is that a Pareto-optimal solution is *not* very likely as long as the seller has a strong interest in hiding his true costs and his acceptance of a Pareto-optimal quantity would reveal his true costs. Hence, in the situation involved here, e.g. an agent is uncertain about the production costs of the manufacturer, the Wicksell model might very well be of greater interest than a model establishing a Pareto-optimal outcome.

(c) The Wicksell Model in "Marginal Intersection Model Situations"

The last point is of a more theoretical nature, but it shows that the Wicksell model will "beat" the "marginal intersection" model (Bowley's third model) in those situations where this model is applicable, e.g. where the bilateral monopoly situation is handled by a mediator using some kind of market simulation procedure.[1]

An important problem inherent in the marginal intersection model is as follows. If the seller, who we assume is a manufacturer, knows that the solution of the marginal intersection model will be reached, he will find it advantageous to increase his costs. The seller can then obtain a solution for a quantity $q' < q^0$ in e.g. the following way: immediately prior to the start of the bargaining, he announces a new wage rate which increases rapidly with production after total production has reached $q' - \varepsilon$. The new wage rate is such that TC remains unchanged for $q < q' - \varepsilon$. and $MC = MR$ for $q = q'$. Then the solution according to the marginal intersection model is that an agreement will be reached on q'. Since ε is very small, TC is virtually the same at this quantity as it was before the cost increase. The optimal value of q' for the seller is hence approximately the q at which the seller maximized π_S—with the original cost functions—under the restriction that $P = p + qp'$, i.e. we get $q' = q^w$ and $P = P^w$, that is the Wicksell solution. Hence if the institutional assumptions are those commonly connected with the application of the marginal intersection model, then the Wicksell solution will be obtained.

---

[1] See Ståhl (1972, p. 217).

References

Allen, R. G. D.: *Mathematical economics*. London, 1937.
Arvidsson, G.: *Internal transfer negotiations*. Stockholm, 1973.
Böhm-Bawerk, E.: *Capital and interest*, vol. II, Bk. III. Positive theory of capital, part. B, ch. II, London, 1959. (First published in German 1884–1889.)
Boulding, K. E.: *A reconstruction of economics*. New York, 1950.
Bowley, A. L.: *The mathematical groundwork of economics*. Oxford, 1924.
Bowley, A. L.: On bilateral monopoly. *Economic Journal*, 1928, pp. 651–659.
Coddington, A.: *Theories of the bargaining process*. London, 1968.
Coddington, A.: Bargaining as a decision process. *Swedish Journal of Economics*, 1973, pp. 397–405.
Cournot, A.: *Recherches sur les principes mathématiques de la théorie des richesses*. Paris, 1838.
Edgeworth, F.: *Mathematical physics*. London, 1881.
Fellner, W.: Prices and wages under bilateral monopoly. *Quarterly Journal of Economics*, 1947, pp. 503–532.
Fouraker, L. E.: Professor Fellner's bilateral monopoly theory. *Southern Economic Journal*, 1957, pp. 182–189.
Fouraker, L. E. & Siegel, S.: *Bargaining behavior*. New York, 1963.
Grubbström, R. W.: *Experimental inquiries into the validity of the economic equation of motion* (Mimeographed). Stockholm, 1972.
Hicks, J. R.: Annual survey of economic theory. The theory of monopoly. *Econometrica*, 1935, pp. 16 ff.
Machlup, F. & Taber, M.: Bilateral monopoly, successive monopoly, and vertical integration. *Economica*, 1960, pp. 101–119.
Menger, C.: *Grundsätze der Volkwirtschaftslehre*. Wien, 1871.
Pareto, V.: *Cours d'economie politique*. Lausanne, 1896.
Schenitzki, D.: *Bargaining group decision making and the attainment of maximum joint outcome*. (Unpublished doctoral dissertation.) Minneapolis, 1962. (Reviewed in Kelley, H. H., Interaction process and the attainment of maximum joint profit. In Messick, S. & Brayfield, A. H. (eds.), *Decision and choice: Contributions of Sidney Siegel*, New York, 1964).
Schneider, E.: *Pricing and equilibrium*. London, 1952.
Schumpeter, J.: Zur Einführung der folgenden Arbeit Knut Wicksells. *Archiv für Sozialwissenschaften und Sozialpolitik*, 1927, pp. 248–251.
Schumpeter, J.: *History of economic analysis*. New York, 1954.
Siegel, S. & Fouraker, L. E.: *Bargaining and group decision making*. New York, 1960.
Ståhl, I.: *En modell för bilateralt monopol vid ofullständig information på köparsidan*. (Mimeographed.) Stockholm, 1965.
Ståhl, I.: *En experimentell test av en modell för bilateralt monopol vid ofullständig information på köparsidan*. (Mimeographed.) Stockholm, 1966.
Ståhl, I.: *Studier i det bilaterala monopolets teori*. (Mimeographed.) Stockholm, 1967.
Ståhl, I.: *Bargaining theory*. Stockholm, 1972.
Tintner, G.: Note on the problem of bilateral monopoly. *Journal of Political Economy*, 1939, pp. 263–270.
Wicksell, K.: Matematisk nationalekonomi. Recension av Bowley, A. L., The mathematical groundwork of economics, Oxford, 1924. *Ekonomisk tidskrift 27*, 1925, pp. 103–25.
German translation in *Archiv für Sozialwissenschaft und Sozialpolitik 58*, 1927, pp. 252–81.
English translation in Wicksell, K., *Selected papers on economic theory* (ed. with an introduction by Erik Lindahl). London & Cambridge, Mass., 1958. 292 p.
Wicksell, K.: Zur Zinstheorie (Böhm-Bawerks dritter Grund) in Die *Wirtschaftstheorie der Gegenwert*. Hrsg. von H. Mayer et al. Bd. 3, Wien, 1928, pp. 199–209.

WICKSELL EFFECTS AND RESWITCHINGS OF TECHNIQUE IN CAPITAL THEORY*

Luigi L. Pasinetti

Università Cattolica del Sacro Cuore, Milan, Italy

Abstract

The difficulties in traditional capital theory, which have recently given rise to the reswitching of technique debate, are traced back to Knut Wicksell's analysis of capital accumulation and to his discussions with Gustaf Åkerman. Some of the later discussions on the "Wicksell effect" are reviewed. It is shown that the separation of price changes from physical changes—which was proposed by David Champernowne and Trevor Swan in a polemical argument with Joan Robinson—is not possible, in general. It is concluded that Wicksell's original arguments were correct, although incomplete. When "by the last portion of capital is meant an increase in social capital", then not only is the marginal productivity of capital unrelated to the rate of profit in any predictable way—as Wicksell pointed out; it no longer has any useful role to play.

I. Introduction

The controversy on capital theory which flared up in the 1960s (see Pasinetti *et al.*, 1966) may still be open to conflicting interpretations. One result, however, is conclusively established: the inverse monotonic relation between the rate of profit and the amount of capital per man (and the inverse monotonic relation between the rate of profit and capital per unit of output), which the whole traditional capital theory had always taken for granted, must be abandoned. In general, such a relation does not exist.

The participants in the recent debate on capital theory have arrived at this conclusion by starting from the "reswitching of technique" phenomenon which emerged from Sraffa's (1960) model of production. It can be shown, however, that the roots of the difficulties which led to the recent discussions can be traced back to the analysis of capital accumulation carried out by Knut Wicksell (1934).

II. The Wicksell Effect

One striking feature of Wicksell's treatment of capital is his refutation of a basic theorem which he attributed to von Thünen. The theorem stated that,

---
* Financial support from C.N.R., Rome (C T 73.00412-10) is gratefully acknowledged. Thanks are also due to Professor Björn Thalberg for criticism and comments.

under conditions of perfect competition, the marginal productivity of capital is equal to the rate of interest. Wicksell objected that when "by the last portion of capital is meant an increase in *social* capital", von Thünen's theorem is no longer correct, because an increase in the capital stock brings about a change in factor prices and, therefore, in the unit in which capital itself is measured (see Wicksell, 1934, p. 180; cf. also pp. 147 and ff.). To prove this statement Wicksell gave a simple example which has been largely used in the later economic literature with only slight modifications—the example of ripening wine or of growing timber—in which there is a technical function of the point-input point-output type, the input being labor and the output being a final product, wine or timber. Wicksell's example is worth recalling. Without going into detail, here are his equations (Wicksell, 1934, pp. 178–180):

$$Q = Nf(t), \qquad (1)$$

$$wN = Qe^{-\varrho t}, \qquad (2)$$

$$\varrho = \frac{f'(t)}{f(t)}, \qquad (3)$$

$$K = wN \int_0^t e^{\varrho x} dx = \frac{Q - wN}{\varrho}, \qquad (4)$$

where Q is the quantity of, let us say, timber produced each "year"; N is the number of workers; ϱ is the rate of interest; t is time; w is the wage rate in terms of timber; K is the value of the stock of capital, expressed in terms of the final product (timber).

By considering K and N as given, Wicksell pointed out that the system gives solutions for Q, ϱ, w, t. By then differentiating Q with respect to K, he obtained the following expression:

$$\frac{dQ}{dK} = \varrho + (K - Nwt)\frac{d\varrho}{dK}, \qquad (5)$$

and since $d\varrho/dK < 0$ and $K > Nwt$, then $dQ/dK < \varrho$, that is the marginal productivity of capital is always lower than the rate of interest (which, in Wicksell's analysis of capital, is always taken to be equal to the rate of profit). This is what Wicksell intended to prove.

The reasons for this inequality were illustrated by Wicksell himself by means of a diagram (see Fig. 1). Consider two positions of equilibrium A and B, with the same technical function $f(t)$, the same number of workers, but different amounts of capital (the two areas $OTAQ''$ and $OT'BQ'$). The difference between the two amounts of capital can be split into two parts: a first part (the area $ABT'T$) which is due to a longer period of production and a second part (the area $Q''Q'BA$) which is due to differences in "factor prices" (a higher wage rate only partially compensated by a lower interest rate). This second

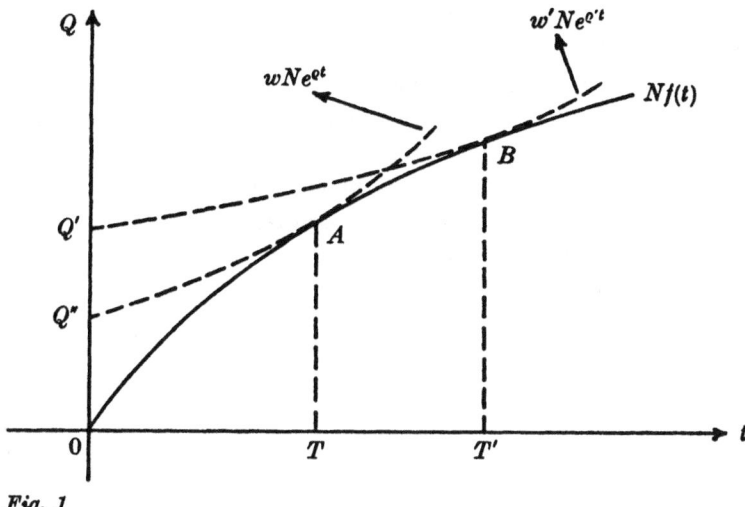

Fig. 1

part represents what, in the economic literature, has later been called the *Wicksell effect*.

As is well known, this analysis did not remain unchallenged for very long. Toward the end of Wicksell's life, another Swedish economist, Gustaf Åkerman, encountered the same problem in a book on capital theory (Åkerman, 1923). Wicksell reviewed that book and, in doing so, he gave a remarkable mathematical reformulation of what has become known as "Åkerman's problem". In this context, Wicksell used a different example,[1] which is also worth recalling. First the problem of making capital goods is considered—in the example, axes—which are assumed to be made by unassisted labor and to be the same in all respects except in their durability. More precisely, if more labor is employed to make an axe, the axe is more durable, according to a technical function $l = \gamma n^\nu$ (where l is labor, n is lifetime of an axe, and γ, ν are positive constants). At this point a second problem is added of combining axes, during their lifetime, with *other labor* in order to produce a commodity for final consumption. In this connection a neoclassical type of production function of the following form is assumed: $Q = aM^\alpha C^\beta$ (where Q is the quantity of final commodity, M is the number of workers producing the final commodity, C is the stock of axes in existence and a, α, β are positive constants). By working through this example, an expression corresponding to eq. (5) can be obtained, of the following form:

$$\frac{dQ}{dK} = h\varrho, \tag{6}$$

---

[1] See Wicksell's "Mathematical Analysis of Dr Åkerman's Problem", which first appeared in *Ekonomisk Tidskrift*, 1923; then reproduced in Wicksell (1934, pp. 274–299).

where h is a complicated formula which depends on many factors and may turn out to be either higher or lower than unity.[1]

This result came, in one way, as very pleasing to the 72-year-old Wicksell, who could find confirmation of his earlier proposition about a divergence between marginal productivity of capital and rate of interest. But, in another way, the result was also very puzzling to him,[2] as it showed that the divergence could be either in the direction he had earlier pointed out (what was later called a *direct* Wicksell effect) or in the opposite direction (a Wicksell effect *in reverse*) depending on the relation between the production of capital goods and the production of consumption goods.

III. The Champernowne–Swan Fable

The full implications of Wicksell's analysis did not become clear for some time. Most of the formal treatments that followed remained tied down to Wicksell's specific examples. Among economists it continued to be believed, as Figure 1 seemed to indicate, that a change from a situation such as A to another situation such as B, in which there is a lower rate of profit and a higher wage rate, would *always* entail an *increase* in the capital stock, and this increase could be split up in two parts: (i) an increase in physical capital; and (ii) a revaluation of the capital stock. The only modification brought by "Åkerman's problem" was a recognition that, in some cases, there might be a devaluation of the existing capital stock (a Wicksell effect in reverse) instead of a revaluation.

It was natural, within this frame of mind, to tend to look at the Wicksell effect (whether direct or in reverse) as a sort of complication which blurs an otherwise clear picture, without affecting it fundamentally. And it is no surprise that proposals began to be made for eliminating the "Wicksell effect" altogether from the relations concerning capital.

Trevor Swan (1956), in an article criticizing Joan Robinson (1954, 1956) for worrying too much about Wicksell, used an example in which capital is assumed to consist of homogeneous physical units—something like meccanosets. He showed that, in such a model, physical changes are separable from price changes. He then went on the claim that the same separation should be made for the general case. He concluded that the "Wicksell effect is nothing but an inventory revaluation" (Swan, 1956, p. 355), and should simply be eliminated from our theoretical elaborations.

---

[1] Because it deals with two different technical functions, this second example cannot be represented graphically in the same way as the previous one.

[2] Here is Wicksell's comment: "I cannot enter now on the explanation of this very puzzling formula [our formula (6), in which $h \leq 1$]; presumably it belongs to the sphere of 'dynamic' theory, where we cannot confine ourselves to the comparison of different equilibria, but must also study the transition from one to the other" (Wicksell, 1934, p. 293). But such a remark is out of place. Expression (6) is no more or no less 'dynamic' or 'static' than expression (5).

The technical device for doing so had been provided by David Champernowne (1954) in the form of a "chain index". Champernowne's idea was that, in an economic system in which there is a finite number of techniques, each of which is characterized by specific and heterogeneous capital goods, one could order them according to the succession in which they appear on the technological frontier, as the rate of profit decreases (and the wage rate increases). If the techniques, in succession, are called α, β, γ, ..., ω, then one could compare, and add up, the capital goods referring to techniques α and β at those prices which correspond to that particular rate of profit at which α and β are equally profitable. If the rate of profit were to fall (and the wage rate to rise), so that technique β became more profitable than technique α, then the *value* of capital goods would indeed change, but such a change should simply not be recorded. Further falls in the rate of profit and further changes in the value of capital goods should continue *not* to be recorded until the point at which technique β and technique γ become equally profitable. At this new point—and at this point only—computations could be resumed. Again one could compare, and add up, the capital goods referring to technique γ and the capital goods referring to technique β, by weighting them by the prices corresponding to the rate of profit at which β and γ are equally profitable. And so on, from γ to δ, to ... ω, in a chain-like way.[1]

The illusion was thereby created that all the changes due to pure "financial" variations (changes in wage rate and rate of profit, or "Wicksell effects", whether direct or in reverse) had been eliminated, and that what remained was an "index" representing a *physical* measure of capital. The result seemed to be important; for, in terms of this index, the ratio of the increment of net product to the increment of capital is always and necessarily equal to the rate of profit.[2] This was interpreted as a confirmation of the traditional equality of marginal productivity and rate of profit. It looked as if the original von Thünen theorem had been vindicated, and Wicksell had mistaken for something important what was "nothing but an inventory revaluation".

IV. Reswitchings of Technique

The Champernowne-Swan fable (as other fables and parables) came to an end after the recent debate on the reswitching of technique.

We now know that techniques cannot in general be ordered in the way Champernowne proposed. If a technique α is the most profitable technique at a high rate of profit and is then discarded in favor of technique β at a lower rate of profit, it does not necessarily follow that such technique is discarded forever. At a still lower rate of profit, technique α might well switch back on the technological frontier to be once again the most profitable

---
[1] See Appendix 1.
[2] Cf. Pasinetti (1969, pp. 529–531).

technique.[1] When this happens, Champernowne's chain index leads us straight into contradiction. The capital goods of technique α are attributed a certain measurement when the economic system switches from technique α to technique β, and then are attributed a *different* measurement (though they are *the same physical goods*) when the economic system switches back to technique α.[2] Champernowne's chain index (which was proposed as a measurement of capital purified of all Wicksell effects, i.e. as a physical measurement) is thus revealed *not* to be any physical measurement at all.[3]

Champernowne tried to escape by making the assumption that cases such as those involving the reswitching of technique do not occur.[4] But this would mean closing our eyes in order not to see. The contradiction is clearly not due to the phenomenon of reswitching of technique as such. The reswitching of technique simply makes us see the contradiction openly!

The hard fact is that a physical measurement of capital, though of course possible in those cases in which it is made possible by assumption—by assuming capital to consist of physically homogeneous capital goods (as in Wicksell's example of wood growing in the forest or in Swan's example of identical meccano-sets)—is not possible in general, when the capital goods used with the different techniques are heterogeneous. And if it is not possible in general to obtain an unambiguous measurement of physical capital, then it is not possible to say what part of any change may be attributed to a physical change and what part of it may be attributed to a price change. Quite simply, when "by capital is meant social capital", a separation of price changes from physical changes is impossible.

It is worth mentioning that Wicksell himself never suggested that such a separation should be attempted. He was right.

V. Should the Rate of Profit be Exogenous?

Knut Wicksell's refutation of von Thünen's theorem on the equality of the marginal productivity of capital and the rate of interest emerges therefore,

---

[1] See Appendix 2.

[2] In the case represented by Fig. 3 in Appendix 2, Champernowne's chain index would assign two *different* measures to the same physical capital goods associated with technique α, according to whether the economic system is at switch point $\bar{\bar{\varrho}}$ or at switch point $\bar{\varrho}$.

Incidentally, this also reveals how misleading Joan Robinson's diagram of Fig. 2, Appendix 1, is. I have argued at length elsewhere (Pasinetti, 1966, p. 524n) that such diagram cannot in fact be used, except in very special cases; the reason being that when the wage rate and the rate of profit change, a change also takes place in the unit in terms of which capital is measured on the horizontal axis. The whole diagram is thereby upset.

[3] What is it then? It is clearly something obtained by taking capital at current prices and deducting from it precisely that amount which makes what remains a "quantity" that satisfies the equality of the marginal productivity and the rate of profit. This seem to be a typical example of what Leontief (1937) once called "implicit theorizing".

[4] In pre-reswitching-of-technique times, Champernowne could argue that "intuition suggests that the excluded case is unrealistic", although candidly admitting that "there is no logical justification for the assumption" (Champernowne, 1954, p. 119)

after the recent discussions, as the very important first step in the correct direction. In terms of our previous relation:

$$\frac{dQ}{dK} = h\varrho, \tag{6}$$

Wicksell proved that, in general, $h \neq 1$. First he found a simple example in which $h < 1$, and then he found that h might well be <1 or >1. His results were correct, though he did not realize how large an iceberg there still was below the tip on which he had stumbled.

We have gone down much deeper today. After the reswitching of technique discussions we know that, in following a decreasing rate of profit on the technological frontier, as we go from one technique to the next, we cannot even be sure of coming to techniques that entail *increases* of output and capital. We might well come to techniques entailing lower outputs and lower amounts of capital per man.[1] In other words, the possibilities are much wider than Wicksell could imagine. As one proceeds to lower and lower rates of profit, not only might h be different from unity, but the ratio $\Delta Q/\Delta K$, of the increments of net product to capital, might even turn out to have a negative numerator and denominator! This means that, if we want to follow a process of increasing capital stock, at current prices, we may not necessarily find a decreasing rate of profit; and if we want to follow a process of decreasing rates of profit, we may not necessarily find an increasing capital stock, at current prices.

These results give some idea of the profound changes that the capital theory which Wicksell inherited from Böhm-Bawerk must undergo. Wicksell's simple model in Section II consists of 4 equations—(1), (2), (3) and (4)—in six unknowns: w, ϱ, t, Q, K, N. Wicksell thought he could make the system determinate by taking N and K as given, the idea being that N and K are exogeneous magnitudes. He thought that, for any given N, accumulation takes place by additions to the capital stock, which bring about increments of output, but less than in proportion—a decreasing marginal productivity of capital and a decreasing rate of profit.

It is precisely this traditional conception of the process of capital accumulation that the results mentioned above reveal to be wanting and, in any case, not to be of general validity. In Wicksell's own simple model, N, by being a physical magnitude, may indeed be taken as exogenously given, but the same cannot be done for K. Wicksell uses K to denote the aggregate stock of capital at current prices; it makes no sense to take it as exogeneously given. To keep the system determinate one must look among the other variables

---

[1] This is precisely what would happen, in a stationary economic system, in the case represented by Fig. 3, Appendix 2. Technique α would entail a higher amount of capital per man and a higher amount of output per man than technique β, at both switch points.

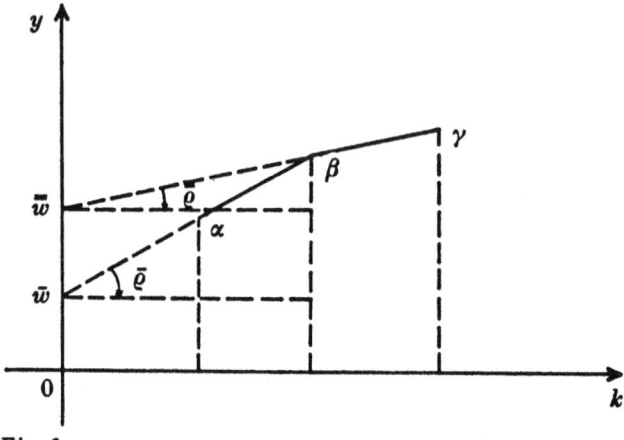

Fig. 2

(Q, t, w, ϱ), to single out the one that is determined exogenously. And, in a long run equilibrium model, the sensible choice to make seems to me to be the rate of profit. Paradoxically, this makes the rate of profit entirely unrelated to "capital". But is this not precisely what we find in production models *à la* Leontief–Sraffa–von Neumann?

We may, for the moment, simply complete Wicksell's original proposition. "If by the last portion of capital is meant an increase in *social* capital", then not only is the marginal productivity of capital unrelated to the rate of profit in any predictable way; it no longer has any useful role to play.

Appendix 1

Champernowne's analysis (1954) was specifically tailored to fit Joan Robinson's model of capital accumulation through a succession of discrete techniques (α, β, γ, etc.), which were taken as exhibiting increasing capital intensities as the rate of profit decreases. In terms of Joan Robinson's diagrams (an example is given in Fig. 2, where capital per man, k, is on the abscissa and output per man, y, is on the ordinate), Champernowne's chain index would register an increase in the quantity of capital when the economic system moves from technique α to technique β at (constant) factor prices ($\bar{w}$, $\bar{\varrho}$) and also when the economic system moves from technique β to technique γ at (constant) factor prices ($\bar{\bar{w}}$, $\bar{\bar{\varrho}}$). But the index would *not* register any change when the capital stock changes in value owing to changes in the wage rate from $\bar{w}$ to $\bar{\bar{w}}$ and in the rate of profit from $\bar{\varrho}$ to $\bar{\bar{\varrho}}$.

Appendix 2

The "reswitching of technique" phenomenon is normally shown graphically by plotting the wage rate/rate of profit relations of the various alternative

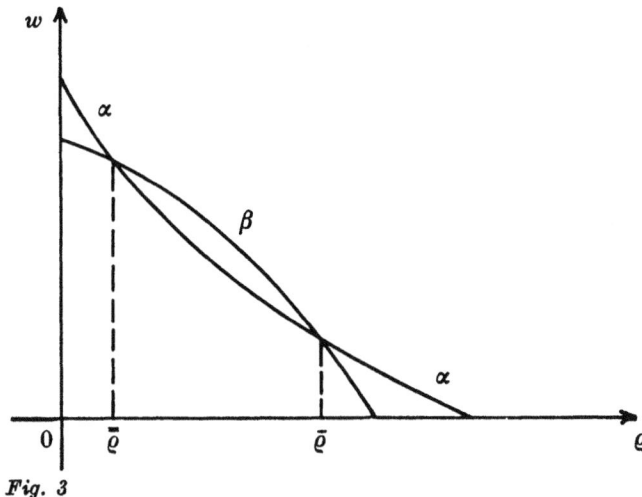

Fig. 3

techniques on the same diagram. As an example see Fig. 3, where two techniques, α and β, are considered. As the rate of profit decreases, the economic system switches from α to β, at rate of profit $\bar{\varrho}$, and then switches back to α, at rate of profit $\bar{\bar{\varrho}}$.

References

Champernowne, David: The production function and the theory of capital: A comment. *Review of Economic Studies 21*, 112–135, 1954.

Leontief, Wassily W.: Implicit theorizing: a methodological criticism of the neo-Cambridge School. *Quarterly Journal of Economics 51*, 337–351, 1937.

Pasinetti, Luigi L. et al.: Paradoxes in capital theory: a symposium. *Quarterly Journal of Economics 80*, 503–583, 1966.

Pasinetti, Luigi L.: Switches of technique and the 'rate of return' in capital theory. *Economic Journal 79*, 508–531, 1969.

Robinson, Joan: The production function and the theory of capital. *Review of Economic Studies 21*, 81–106, 1954.

Robinson, Joan: *The accumulation of capital.* Macmillan, London, 1956.

Sraffa, Piero: *Production of commodities by means of commodities—prelude to a critique of economic theory.* Cambridge University Press, Cambridge, 1960.

Swan, Trevor: Economic growth and capital accumulation. *Economic Record 32*, pp. 334–361, 1956.

Wicksell, Knut: *Lectures on Political Economy,* vol. I, translated from the Swedish by E. Classen and edited by Lionel Robbins, London, Routledge & Kegan Paul Ltd., 1934 (first edition: *Föreläsningar i nationalekonomi* I, Lund, 1901).

Åkerman, Gustaf: *Realkapital und Kapitalzins.* Stockholm, 1923.

WICKSELL AND THE MALTHUSIAN CATASTROPHE

Richard Goodwin

Peterhouse College, Cambridge, England

Abstract

By the use of a simple form of catastrophe theory, an attempt is made to develop an abstract, qualitative analysis of the pure theory of population. The model is constructed in such a way as to emphasize the importance of the problem posed by a very large population subsisting on non-renewable resources. Far from being outmoded, the concerns of Malthus and Wicksell are shown to be potentially present in an acute and special form—overshoot.

I. Introduction

Wicksell is peculiarly relevant to the agonizing reappraisal, now on-going, of economic growth. After 200 years of fitful but persistent growth, grave doubts have arisen about its implications for the future. The people want it; politicians preach it and try to practice it; economists could think of nothing else for the last couple of decades. Until the oil crisis, the future apparently worried no one.

Here is where Wicksell is so apposite. After a scientific training, he at one point read and got the Malthusian message: perceptively he realized that the issues posed required more serious economic analysis than they had received: accordingly he devoted the rest of his life to that task. Thus he soon came under the influence of the New Economics, marginalism, and felt it superior to Malthus and to classical economics generally. It may have been this influence which gradually undermined and ultimately practically eradicated his commitment to neo-Malthusianism. In my view this was a tragedy, and I shall try to explain how and why.

There is the awkward initial question: is neo-classical economic method better than the classical one? One has to ask: better for what? If I may be dogmatic, I would say that marginalism is, in principle, subtler, more sophisticated and, in a sense, truer than classical analysis. It is vastly more complex and goes into details, into the fine structure of the economy. This gain is achieved, however, at a heavy cost: the broad outlines, the central tendencies, the evolution of the whole, all were lost—until Keynes brought something of them back (paying excessive tribute to Malthus in the process).

Wicksell, I feel, sensed that much was being lost and struggled against losing himself in that detail. It was partly for this reason, I think, that, as a student, I preferred him to all other economists. Though he did not shun meticulous logic, he never surrendered to details in the manner of Walras or of Marshall. Nevertheless it is a fact that he did drop the section on demography from the second edition of his final testament, the *Lectures*; he never really carried his analysis of capital beyond the stationary state and simple interest; he relegated the fundamental issue of capital accumulation to a brief and uncharacteristically tentative section of the *Lectures*; and though he remained impressed by Malthus and Ricardo, he seems never to have appreciated the significance of Marx's development of classical economics.

As both Malthus and Wicksell recognized, population is intimately related to production. Demography was and should have remained the province of economists, but they abandoned it, apparently for the simple reason that Malthus's dire predictions were wrong. They failed to notice that the fault lay in the economics more than in the demography. Animal population theory can take the environment and the availability of food as substantially constant, as in the classic Reed-Pearl experiment. That wont do for people: Malthus proposed his crude arithmetic-geometric formula. That wont do either, and so we have, at the very least, to progress to Ricardo's declining marginal product of land.

Thus economics became in the early nineteenth century the dismal science because it predicted a homeostatic feed-back mechanism for the standard of living: no matter how much technology progressed, the population would increase and swamp the increased product. In the long run the level of consumption had always to be at that level which equated births and deaths. This proposition sounds less than inpressive after 200 years in which they have been unequal: nonetheless it remains true that it is inconceivable to have them indefinitely unequal. However, the precise mechanism by which they are equated and when and at what levels of total world population are matters which have escaped the finest analytic meshes. Of course, Malthus always waits in the wings; if some more gentle mechanism fails, there is the final solution of in-finite growth in a finite world.

Malthus's seminal proposition has been falsified for so long because output has been able to keep pace with the population explosion, indeed far to outpace it in many parts of the world. Ultimately the vital question must be posed: can this be a permanent resolution or has the Malthusian spectre only been postponed? The main reason for renewed doubt springs from the distinction between renewable and non-renewable resources. Malthus thought, quite properly for his time, primarily in terms of agriculture. All things which depend for their source on solar energy may be thought of as eternal for all practical purposes. This leads to the Ricardian theory of rent. By contrast such a theory is totally inapplicable to exhaustible resources like oil, uranium, iron, copper, etc. They constitute a completely different and disturbingly perverse situation. The urgency springs from two facts. One is that these resources exist in fixed amounts and once used cannot, for the most part, be used again. The second is that so long as only a small part of the globe experienced the great upsurge of production, the problem did not seem pressing. Beginning with the second half of this century, substantially the whole world is aiming to carry out a similar output explosion. It is for this reason that it is unavoidable to analyze in terms of world output and world population, however unsatisfactory that may be.

The economists abandoned demography to specialist demographers, who have complicated the subject (rightly) without having succeeded in achieving any very satisfactory predictive power. They in turn have abandoned the subject to the historians, which probably is equivalent to giving up hope for a quantitative theory. The historians will no doubt enormously improve the empirical bases of our knowledge of the variety of influences on death and fertility rates, but that any generally valid laws will emerge is open to grave doubt. The defection of economists is to be deplored for the subject really is (apart from the great technical complexities) an economic problem, exactly in the spirit Malthus posed it and Wicksell pursued it. That the problem is one of analyzing the nature of the mechanism by which birth and death rates are equalized, has been amply shown in the simpler cases of animal populations.

If one believes, as I do, that there could eventually be some sort of spectacular collapse of our industrial civilization, then the subject is of great interest, even though it may be remote in time. The fact that the problem is of an intractable complexity does not mean that it will go away. Economists have a bad record here; they have ignored and attacked the assorted scientists, business men, and crackpots who have warned of the danger; they have done so on the sound grounds that no one can predict the economic future (they should know; look at their own disastrous record). But this is a sword that cuts two ways: if we cannot predict disaster, we cannot predict that there will be none. The nineteenth century belief in perpetual progress appears to have found its last resting place with economists. The multiple disasters of this century, which have cooled the faith in the future, seem only to have awakened it in economists.

What is required is an analysis both qualitative and global—qualitative in not resting on specific, quantitative functions and global in the sense of encompassing large variations in the quantities, and hence not really suitable for linearization (though I shall have to make use of such for simplicity of analysis). Viewed secularly, our society is in continuous, strong disequilibrium and it will, like all previous societies, disappear in the course of time. A good candidate for analyzing this potential decay is demographic analysis which may suggest how and why, though scarcely when, it may disappear. Though we have very little firm empirical knowledge about the factors determining net fertility and death rates, nonetheless one can reach some global conclusions without any very precise relationships. The most obvious example is that, without knowing anything, one can say that birth and death rates cannot be permanently unequal. I shall use the crudest of concepts with the limited aim of getting something like an aerial view of the terrain that lies ahead. This involves using a single world output, a single world natural resource, crude birth and death rates, thus ignoring net rates, age composition, dependency and participation rates, national and regional differences. Output per head will be taken to represent standard of living with no regard for the effects of growth rates.

II. Population and Resources: The Prey and the Predator Mechanism

Suppose that, for whatever reason, average birth and death rates have been both equal and constant, so that population, x, has, with temporary excursions, remained constant.

$$\dot{x}/x = b - d = 0.$$

If there occurs a small exogenous, parametric change which puts one or the other of b or d above or below the other, then the behaviour of population becomes qualitatively different; in the one case numbers increase without limit; in the other the species disappears. This is to be contrasted with the case in which, with b unequal to d, there is a small change: the behaviour is altered quantitatively but not qualitatively. With b and d equal the system is said to be structurally unstable—to be sharply distinguished from the ordinary dynamical instability. Where such a small parametric change gives rise to a clear bifurcation in behaviour is the simplest example of what René Thom (1975) has christened a catastrophe, a designation peculiarly appropriate to population theory.

The case of $b > d$ corresponds to a species newly introduced into an area with a given environment of edible plant life. However, this regime is untenable for any prolonged period: there must be a mechanism for bringing the two rates into equality. With a constant energy source (solar), producing a constant flow of food, there will be a population, $\bar{x}$, which just consumes the annual output of food. Any larger x will lead to over-grazing and a falling per capita food supply, with rising d and possibly falling b. Assuming a linear approximation, the result is the basic population equation, the logistic:

$$\dot{x}/x = A - Bx,$$

giving $x = A/B$ for $\dot{x} = 0$. Though a bit too simple for human populations, this does illustrate the powerful logic of Malthus.

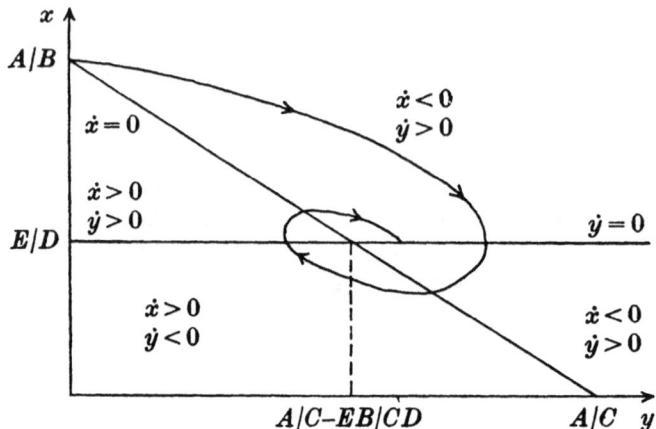

Fig. 1

This example also permits of a slightly more interesting example of a catastrophe. Suppose into this garden of Eden, a small number of human pairs is introduced, and that they are meat-eating hunter-fisher folk. The death rate of the prey now depends both on the environment and on the number of men, y. x now denotes the stock animals and y the human population. Then, keeping to growth-rate linear relations,

$\dot{x}/x = A - Bx - Cy$,

yielding, for $\dot{x}=0$,

$x = A/B - (C/B)y$.

The men have only the prey as food supply, a variable one dependent on their own numbers, hence

$\dot{y}/y = Dx - E$,

giving, for $\dot{y}=0$, $x = E/D$. As shown in the accompanying diagram, the vector field consists of 4 areas along with the two coordinate axes. Prior to the appearance of man, the animal population, however disturbed by, say, climate, is confined to the x axis and will be tending always towards the stable equilibrium point, A/B. The introduction of a small number of human beings constitutes a catastrophe which leads to a completely different behaviour of the animal population. The human population increases rapidly in exceptionally favourable circumstances but gradually decelerates as its own growth reduces its prey. Once the predators numbers have fallen sufficiently, the animals begin again to increase. Thus the two populations, interdependent both complementarily and competitively, oscillate out of phase in decreasing swings towards a stable focus.[1] The result is that a very small initial change

[1] The system can be shown to be globally stable and locally asymptotically stable.

causes the animals to move away from the point A/B, never to return. Parallel to this, the human population is launched into a large, unsteady growth towards a new equilibrium level, $(A/C)-(EB/CD)$.

The resulting cyclical behaviour is a variant of the famous prey-predator mechanism investigated and solved by Volterra (and independently by Lotka). The theory was generalized by Kolmogoroff (1936) and shown to yield useful qualitative results for general, non-linear functions, i.e.

$\dot{x}/x = f(x, y)$

$\dot{y}/y = g(x, y).$

Knowing only certain qualitative characteristics of the functions, e.g. slope and position, one can describe the nature of the resulting behaviour.

Pursuing this 'stylized history', man discovers a superior technology for exploiting solar energy by settled agriculture, it being much more efficient to feed on plants than to feed on animals who feed on plants. As the grazing lands are turned to cultivation, the animals partially or totally disappear and man becomes subject to a growth law similar to that previously faced by the animals. There will be a certain population $\bar{y} > (A/C)-(EB/CD)$, which will consume the annual produce, beyond which there will be a falling consumption per head. In linear form,

$\dot{y}/y = A - By.$

III. Population and Resources: The Mechanism with Exhaustible Prey

Some such stable situation lasted for a long time, perhaps with a slow rise of A. Then came the industrial revolution of the eighteenth to twentieth centuries. This constituted a catastrophe in the sense that it altered both qualitatively and quantitatively the behaviour and structural relations of population and output. The Malthusian mechanism was only noticed when it ceased to operate; the system changed from dynamical stability to dynamical instability. To put a complex matter simply—the death rate was reduced whilst the birth rate was not, thus ending the mechanism which had kept them substantially equal. As is well understood, the same scientific revolution which reduced the death rate, also led to increased output per head by the use of stored up solar energy to replace human and animal energy, along with the massive use of various minerals. For present purposes the essential feature of this process was the use, on an accelerating scale, of exhaustible resources.

The Malthusian trap has been evaded but only in a manner which carries ominous implications for the future. With a rising standard of living the implacable Malthusian mechanism is simply non-existent. The birth rate is falling in many countries but the mechanism by which it may ultimately be equated to the death rate is complex and uncertain, and highly unlikely to behave according to past behaviour. But even if in the course of the next century, the two do come into equality, there will be the enormously swollen population and the still more enormously swollen rate of production which will be sucking up non-renewable, finite resources at a correspodingly gigantic rate. Thus the essential logic of the Malthusian problem is posed in a situation quite different from that of constant resources based on solar energy. This is the prey-predator mechanism with the vital difference that the prey, once consumed will not regenerate, even when the predator population is decimated for lack of sustenance. A simple analogue is provided by the so-called Dutch elm disease. A single shipment of timber introduced into England a small number of the carrier beetles. By now there are thousands of millions of these beetles destroying at an increasing rate the elm population on which they depend. As the elms disappear so also will the beetle that uses them. It is a clear case of a small parametric change leading to total, or near total, disappearance of one population, in parallel with an enormous growth and eventual disappearance of another.

The serious predictions of a difficult future for mankind have thus far come from scientists and an assortment of practical and impractical men. This is partly because of the irresponsibility of economists, who have ignored the world economic problem and restricted themselves to particular countries. Scientists are accustomed to working with relationships specified by numerically given parameters—parameters which will hold under very diverse circumstances. By contrast, economists have no 'universal' constants. Consequently the efforts at prediction by scientists have been understandably greeted with disbelief. What I want to do is to keep to very simple, non-quantitative assumptions, which are, I hope, empirically valid in a rough way, and then to see if it is not possible to arrive at some substantive conclusions from these very 'weak' assumptions.

Suppose that there is a single entity, resources, which may be divided into renewable, $\bar{n}$, and non-renewable, n, so that the total is $n' = \bar{n} + n$. Assume that the human population can similarly be divided into $y' = \bar{y} + y$. In reality, of course, the two types of productivity and associated populations are thoroughly inter-mingled. y may be thought of as the difference between the population sustainable by all resources and that sustainable by solar derived sources alone. The Malthusian mechanism applies to $\bar{y}$ and I shall make the heroic assumption that the scientific revolution, which unlocked the riches of the earth's crust, has its full effect on the $\bar{y}$ population from the start. Therefore $\dot{\bar{y}}/\bar{y} = A - B\bar{y}$, with its permanent equilibrium level at A/B. The rate of growth of y is taken to be positively related to n and negatively to y. Thus in simple, linear form, $\dot{y}/y = Dn - Ey$, whilst $\dot{n} = -Cy$. Initially y is very small and n very large. By definition both n and y are non-negative. The evolution of such

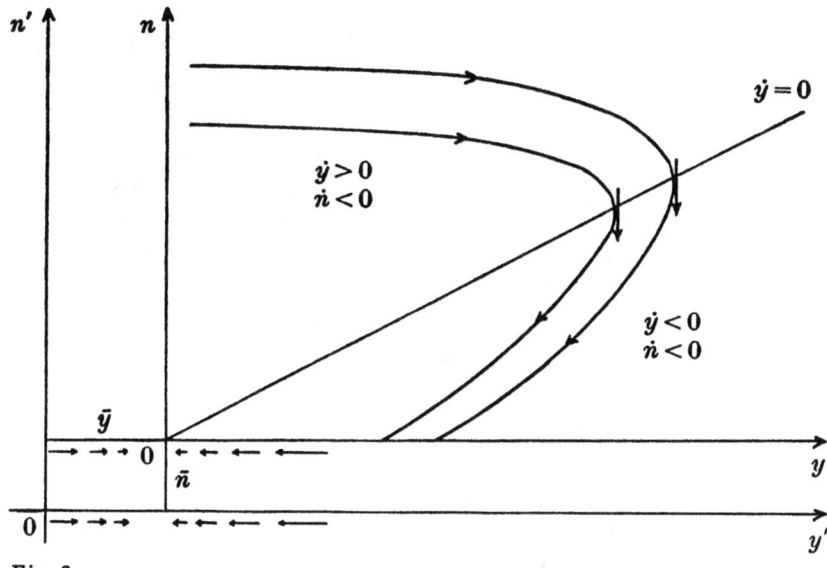

Fig. 2

a system can then be represented, with no attempt at accuracy or scale, as in Fig. 2.

Equilibrium states for n and y are given by $n=(E/D)y$ and $y=0$. The proportional growth of y decelerates from the start but its magnitude first grows and then declines as the size of y begins to have an effect on resources and hence the standard of living. This sequence necessarily continues until $Dn=Ey$ and the population has ceased to grow. At this point, however, the depletion rate of resources is at its maximum. The subsequent decline in y eases the rate of depletion but will not avoid ultimate exhaustion. y then becomes hyper-Malthusian, dying off at an accelerating rate, but this cannot be taken literally; it only points to the unreality of the separation of the two populations as well as of the linearity assumption. The system exhibits global asymptotic stability.

IV. Conclusions

The details of this simple model cannot possibly represent the actual future course of events; it is only meant to reveal clearly certain dominating elements. The assumption of linearity is clearly unsatisfactory and is only defensible in order to make easily intelligible the central features of the process. Secondly, there is almost certain to be hysteresis in the sense that the decline will not obey the same rules as the ascent, for two quite distinct reasons. People do not react symmetrically to rises and to falls. Secondly, the advances in technology, primarily medical, will not entirely be lost in the decline, thus changing the causal relations.

The truly daunting complexity of the problem has the effect that no responsible experts ever face it. The aim of this model, with all its crude oversimplification is to bring out the serious possible consequences of two undeniable facts: the accelerating depletion of a finite stock of resources and the unavoidably huge population dependent on that shrinking stock. No one can say that this debacle must happen but by the same token no one can deny that it may happen. It is possible, but by no means certain, that some remarkable succession of technological advances will continue to circumvent the Malthusian Devil. What is quite certain is that our civilization will depend increasingly on a technology of an ever more complex and all-embracing sort. This looks like meaning an ever diminishing amount of both freedom and democracy.

In a remarkable paper on Malthus, the British astrophysicist Sir Fred Hoyle (1963), argues that the resolution of the population-output explosion will come not through direct impoverishment, but rather as a consequence of the requisite, highly developed technology and organization. The society, resting on such a complex, delicate structure, becomes increasingly vulnerable to social conflict, violence, pollution and ecological imbalance, with the consequence that "... there will be a series of organizational breadowns, or catastrophes, occasioned by overpopulation.". This would present an alternative, but even more precipitious and drastic, collapse.

Some sort of optimal control of population could conceivably offer a much less disastrous course of events: the obsession of the public, of the politicians, of the economists, with growth makes such a solution unlikely. Moreover the feeble results of such efforts as have been made is not encouraging. As long ago as the turn of the century, Wicksell (1977) wrote: "For my own part I have gradually reached the conviction that this optimum population has already been considerably exceeded in our own country as in all the countries of Europe, so that the road to increased prosperity does not lie in any further increase of population but rather in an energetic reduction of the population, continued through decades." In view of what we now know of present and projected world population, one wonders what he would have to say now.

References

Hoyle, F.: A contradiction in the argument of Malthus. Univ. of Hull, 1963.

Kolmogoroff, A.: Sulla teoria di volterra della lotta per l'Esistenza. *Giornale dell-'Istituto degli Attuari*, Gennaio, 1936.

Thom, R.: *Structural stability and morphogenesis*. 1975.

Wicksell, K.: The theory of population, its composition and changes. Translated by Göran Ohlin, in *Some Unpublished Works*, Lund, 1977.

THE LONG-RUN RATE OF PROFIT IN AN ECONOMY WITH NATURAL RESOURCE SCARCITY*

Michael Hoel

University of Oslo, Oslo, Norway

Abstract

According to Knut Wicksell, two important factors which prevent the rate of profit from declining towards zero in an economy with positive saving are labor growth and technical progress. This paper analyzes the effect of these factors and the economy's saving propensity on the long-run rate of profit in an economy with a scarce non-renewable natural resource. The existence of natural resource scarcity depresses the long-run rate of profit. However, the sensitivity of this rate of profit to labor growth and technical progress is the same for economies without and with natural resource scarcity.

I. Introduction

As several economists before him, Knut Wicksell was interested in the long-run development of the accumulation of capital and of the rate of profit. In his *Lectures* (Wicksell, 1928, Ch. IV), he discussed various reasons why members of a society save part of their income and thereby augment the capital stock of the economy, and how this saving might depend on the market rate of interest, which under certain assumptions is equal to the rate of profit. In particular, he gave a critical discussion of some views expressed by Gustav Cassel (1903). According to Cassel, capital accumulation would gradually make the rate of profit and the rate of interest decline. This in turn would undermine the incentive for saving, so that saving and capital accumulation would eventually stop, and the economy would reach a stationary situation with a positive, although low, rate of profit.

Wicksell did not agree with Cassel's view of capital accumulation and the development of the rate of profit. His main objection concerned Cassel's idea about why people saved some of their income. Wicksell maintained that people's saving was not necessarily a declining function of the rate of interest. In particular, he pointed out that one may well have positive saving as long

* I would like to thank Richard Goodwin for critical comments on an earlier version of this paper.

as the rate of interest is positive. Such a development would gradually make the rate of profit approach zero in an economy with a stationary technology and labor force. After having mentioned this possibility, Wicksell gave several reasons (other than Cassel's) as to why the rate of profit may stop falling before it reaches zero. According to him, the most important reasons for this are the growth of the labor force and technical progress. Both of these two factors may offset the negative effect of an increasing capital stock on the rate of profit, so that the economy may follow a development where the rate of profit is constant in spite of the occurrence of capital accumulation.

The long-run development of the rate of profit may be analyzed by means of various types of models of capital and growth. One of the simplest models that can be used is an aggregate neoclassical growth model, often called the Solow–Swan model. This model is used in Hoel (1975) to analyze the effects of the economy's propensity to save, the growth of the labor force and technical progress, on the long-run rate of profit. This analysis is extended here to include the treatment of natural resources. Economists have become increasingly aware of the fact that a realistic long-run analysis of growth and growth-related topics should give explicit attention to the scarcity of natural resources. This paper investigates how the existence of a scarce non-renewable natural resource affects the long-run rate of profit.

A model with no natural resource scarcity is treated briefly in Section II. A growth model with natural resource scarcity is analyzed in Section III, which is the main section of the paper. Some of the results obtained here are compared with the corresponding results from the simple model presented in Section II. Finally, some concluding comments are made in Section IV.

II. No Natural Resource Scarcity

A growth model which does not take natural resource scarcity into account is the following simple Solow–Swan model:

$$Y = F(K, L), \qquad (2.1)$$

$$\dot{K} = sY, \qquad (2.2)$$

$$L(t) = L_0 e^{\sigma t}, \qquad (2.3)$$

where Y is output, K is the capital stock and L is labor measured in efficiency units (time references for all variables are omitted in most instances to simplify notation). The production function is homogeneous of degree one, concave, and has positive marginal productivities of capital and labor. The saving assumption implied by (2.2), where s is exogenous and constant, is not very satisfactory. In particular, it in no way serves justice to Knut Wicksell who, in his work referred to in Section I, discusses several factors which make

K/Y non-autonomous in a developing economy. However, models with simple saving assumptions such as (2.2) do give us a rough idea of how the evaluation of future consumption compared with present consumption affects some of the variables we are interested in, i.e. the long-run rate of profit in the present case.

Labor grows exogenously at the constant rate $n \geqslant 0$, and labor augmenting technical progress takes place at the constant rate $m \geqslant 0$. The growth rate g in (2.3) is therefore given by $g = m+n$, and we shall distinguish between the two cases $g > 0$ and $g = 0$.

Denoting the wage rate (per unit of labor efficiency) by w, we can define the rate of profit π as total non-wage income divided by the value of the capital stock. Choosing our aggregate good as the *numéraire*, we therefore have

$$\pi = \frac{Y - wL}{K}. \qquad (2.4)$$

In a competitive economy we have $F_L = w$, so that (2.4) implies

$$\pi = F_K, \qquad (2.5)$$

i.e. the rate of profit is equal to the marginal productivity of capital, which in turn must be equal to the market rate of interest in our one good competitive economy.

Defining $k = K/L$ and $f(k) = F(k, 1)$, our model (2.1)–(2.3) may be written as

$$\dot{k} = sf(k) - gk, \qquad (2.6)$$

and (2.5) implies that

$$\pi = f'(k). \qquad (2.7)$$

Let us first consider the case where $g > 0$. From (2.6) it is clear that with suitable conditions on the production function, k approaches the steady-state value $\bar{k}$ given by

$$sf(\bar{k}) = g\bar{k}. \qquad (2.8)$$

The steady-state value of the rate of profit is

$$\bar{\pi} = f'(\bar{k}). \qquad (2.9)$$

When $k(t) = \bar{k}$, the rate of profit will be constant, while Y, K and L all grow at the rate g. The wage rate w will be constant, but wages per unit of labor (in natural units) will grow at the rate $m \geqslant 0$.

For any given production function, it is clear that $\bar{\pi}$ depends only on g/s. From (2.8) and (2.9) we see that

$$El.\left(\bar{\pi} : \frac{g}{s}\right) = f'' \cdot \frac{\bar{k}}{f'} \cdot El.\left(\bar{k} : \frac{g}{s}\right).$$

But from (2.8) we get

$$\left(f'\frac{k}{f}-1\right) El.\left(k:\frac{g}{s}\right) = 1,$$

so that

$$El.\left(\bar{\pi}:\frac{g}{s}\right) = -\frac{kff''}{f'(f-kf')}$$

or

$$El.\left(\bar{\pi}:\frac{g}{s}\right) = \frac{1}{\sigma(k)}, \tag{2.10}$$

where $\sigma(k)$ is the elasticity of substitution. In other words, the lower the elasticity of substitution is, the more sensitive is the long-run rate of profit to the growth rate of labor in efficiency units and the saving rate. For the special case of a Cobb–Douglas production function we have $\sigma(k) \equiv 1$, i.e. the rate of profit will be proportional to g/s. To be more specific, if (2.1) can be written

$$Y = K^a L^{1-a}, \tag{2.1'}$$

where $a \in (0, 1)$, we get $f(k) = k^a$ and

$$\bar{\pi} = a\frac{g}{s}. \tag{2.11}$$

Let us look at a numerical example for the Cobb–Douglas case. Assume that

$$a = 0.3, \quad g = 0.04, \quad s = 0.15 \tag{2.12}$$

where a is the parameter in the production function (2.1'). This numerical example gives a long-run rate of profit equal to 8 %. If the saving rate was 7.5 % instead of 15 % as in (2.12), the long-run rate of profit would be 16 %.

Let us now turn to the case in which $g = 0$. Any positive value of s will then imply that k is always growing, cf. (2.6). With the Cobb–Douglas function (2.1') this will imply that the rate of profit gradually approaches zero, while production, consumption and the wage rate grow along unbounded paths. Such a development corresponds to the possibility mentioned by Wicksell (cf. Section I). Cassel, on the other hand, argued that s would drop to zero once π was sufficiently low, which would give stationary values for all our variables.

III. A Growth Model with Exhaustible Natural Resources

We now assume that the use of a non-renewable scarce resource enters into the production function. Simple aggregate growth models with this property have been analyzed by Dasgupta & Heal (1974), Garg & Sweeney (1976), Hoel (1977), Ingham & Simmons (1975), Solow (1974) and Stiglitz (1974a, b). A simple version of such a model is as follows:

$$Y = F(K, R, L), \tag{3.1}$$

$$\dot{K} = sY, \tag{3.2}$$

$$L(t) = L_0 e^{\sigma t}, \tag{3.3}$$

$$\frac{d}{dt}F_R = F_R \cdot F_K, \tag{3.4}$$

$$\int_0^\infty R(t)\,dt = S_0. \tag{3.5}$$

As before, the production function will be assumed to be homogeneous of degree one. When resource use R enters into the production function, the analysis is simplified greatly by assuming that we have a Cobb–Douglas function:

$$Y = K^a R^b L^c, \tag{3.1'}$$

where $c = 1 - a - b$, and a, b and c are positive.

We use this simplification in the subsequent analysis in spite of several unsatisfactory properties of the Cobb–Douglas function (cf., however, Dasgupta & Heal (1974), Solow (1974) and Stiglitz (1974a), who give reasons as to why the Cobb–Douglas case might be of particular interest in addition to being simple to analyze).

The saving assumption (3.2) is the same as the one we used in Section II. However, when we have a durable asset such as a natural resource stock in the model, the relation (3.2) is particularly dubious. In this case any change in the value of the natural resource will imply a capital gain or loss. These capital gains or losses may well affect the saving behavior of the agents in the economy. This is discussed in detail by Burmeister et al. (1973) in a model with several produced capital goods. Stiglitz (1974b) and Dixit (1976, Ch. 7) mention that satisfactory models of economic growth with natural resources ought to take this point into consideration. The saving assumption (3.2) implicitly assumes that all capital gains are saved in addition to the saving given by a constant fraction of "ordinary" income Y.

Relation (3.5) states that the total resource use is effectively constrained by a given initial resource stock S_0. The condition (3.4) is a requirement of intertemporal efficiency (cf. Weinstein & Zeckhauser, 1974), which will be satisfied in a competitive economy with a full set of future markets. This condition is simply the well-known Hotelling (1931) condition that the resource price $q = F_R$ must rise at a rate equal to the market rate of interest ($= F_K$). The economic interpretation of this is that in a competitive world without uncertainty, individuals must receive the same return from holding their wealth regardless of the form they choose for keeping it (e.g. producible capital or a natural resource stock).

Inserting (3.1) and (3.3) into (3.2) and (3.4) gives us two differential equations in $K(t)$ and $R(t)$. The initial value $K(0)$ is given by the history of the economy, while $R(0)$ is determined so that the resulting path for $R(t)$ satisfies (3.5). Once the paths for $K(t)$ and $R(t)$ are found, the development for $Y(t)$ follows from (3.1) and (3.3).

The rate of profit is defined in a similar way as before:

$$\pi = \frac{Y - wL + \dot{q}S + q\dot{S}}{K + qS}, \tag{3.6}$$

where $q(t)$ is the resource price. The term $\dot{q}S + q\dot{S}$ is the change in value of the resource stock, which must be included in the total non-wage income. Similarly, qS is the value of the resource stock, which must be included in the total wealth. Using $F_R = q$, $F_L = w$, $\dot{S} = -R$ and (3.4), it is easy to verify that also in the present case we get

$$\pi = F_K, \tag{3.7}$$

which as before is equal to the market rate of interest in our one produced good competitive economy.

Using the specification (3.1'), (3.1)–(3.3) gives us

$$\frac{\dot{Y}}{Y} = a\frac{\dot{K}}{K} + b\frac{\dot{R}}{R} + cg, \tag{3.8}$$

$$\frac{\dot{K}}{K} = s\frac{Y}{K}, \tag{3.9}$$

$$\frac{\dot{R}}{R} = \frac{\dot{Y}}{Y} - a\frac{Y}{K}, \tag{3.10}$$

where the last equation follows from (3.3), keeping in mind that $F_R = bY/R$ and $F_K = aY/K$. Defining $x = Y/K$ and using the equations above give us

$$\frac{\dot{Y}}{Y} = \frac{\dot{x}}{x} + sx \tag{3.11}$$

and

$$\dot{x} = -\frac{ab + cs}{1 - b}x^2 + \frac{c}{1 - b}gx. \tag{3.12}$$

The differential equation above has a globally stable stationary solution $\bar{x}$, given by

$$\bar{x} = \frac{c}{ab + cs}g. \tag{3.13}$$

Let us first consider the case in which $g>0$, giving $\bar{x}>0$. When $x(t)=\bar{x}$, output will grow at the rate

$$\frac{\dot{Y}}{Y} = \frac{cs}{ab+cs}g; \tag{3.14}$$

cf. (3.11). In other words, $Y(t)$ and $K(t)$ will have a growth rate which is positive (for $s>0$), but lower than g. From (3.1) this obviously must imply $\dot{R}/R < g$. To be more specific, we see from (3.10), (3.13) and (3.14) that

$$\frac{\dot{R}}{R} = -\frac{(a-s)c}{ab+cs}g. \tag{3.15}$$

It can be shown that a constant saving rate can give an efficient consumption path only if $s<a$; cf. Stiglitz (1974b) or Hoel (1977). This inequality implies that $R(t)$ is declining along a path with $x(t)=\bar{x}$.

The rate of profit is given by $\pi = aY/K$; cf. (3.7) and (3.1′). When $Y/K = x = \bar{x}$ we therefore see from (3.13) that

$$\bar{\pi} = \frac{ac}{ab+cs}g. \tag{3.16}$$

It follows immediately from (3.16) that

$$\bar{\pi} < a\frac{g}{s}, \tag{3.17}$$

where the right-hand side of (3.17) is equal to the expression for the long-run rate of profit in the economy described by the model in Section II; cf. (2.11). It is a somewhat dubious procedure to compare two different economies, one without and one with resource scarcity. If, in spite of this, we make such a comparison, we see from (2.11) and (3.17) that for given values of g and s, $\bar{\pi}$ will be lower in the economy with resource scarcity than in the economy without resource scarcity, at least as long as the marginal elasticity of capital is not smaller in the latter economy than in the resource constrained economy.

In contrast to the cases treated in Section II, g and s enter in a more complicated way than as g/s in (3.16). As before, $\bar{\pi}$ is proportional to g. However, it is clear from (3.16) that the absolute value of the elasticity of $\bar{\pi}$ with respect to s is now smaller than one. In other words, the long-run rate of profit is less sensitive to the saving rate in the case of an exhaustible resource than in the case of no resource constraint.

When $x(t)=\bar{x}$, the resource price $q(t)$ rises by the constant rate $\bar{\pi}$. The wage rate w (i.e. per unit of efficiency labor) will always be equal to cY/L, which will be declining when $x(t)=\bar{x}$. More precisely, it follows from (3.3) and (3.14) that

$$\frac{\dot{w}}{w} = -\frac{ab}{ab+cs}g. \tag{3.18}$$

When there is technical progress, i.e. $n<g$, it is more interesting to study the development of wages per unit of natural labor, given by

$$v = we^{mt} = we^{(g-n)t}. \tag{3.19}$$

Combined with (3.18) this gives us

$$\frac{\dot{v}}{v} = \frac{cs}{ab+cs}g - n, \tag{3.20}$$

or

$$\frac{\dot{v}}{v} = \frac{cs}{ab+cs}m - \frac{ab}{ab+cs}n, \tag{3.21}$$

i.e. the wage rate has a rate of growth equal to a weighted average of technical progress (m) and the growth rate of labor with a negative sign ($-n$). It is clear that

$$\frac{\dot{v}}{v} > 0 \Leftrightarrow \frac{m}{n} > \frac{ab}{cs}. \tag{3.22}$$

From this inequality we see that the critical value of m/n (i.e. the value giving $\dot{v}/v=0$) is lower, the higher s is. However, since $s<a$, it follows from (3.22) that $v(t)$ must be declining if $m<n\,b/c$ regardless of the value of $s<a$ chosen.

From (3.16), (3.21) and $\dot{q}/q=\pi$ we can conclude that a higher saving rate gives a lower long-run rate of profit, a slower rise in the resource price, and a faster growth (or slower decline) of wages per worker.

Let us look at a numerical example similar to (2.12):

$$a = 0.25, \quad b = 0.15, \quad c = 0.60, \quad g = 0.04, \quad s = 0.15. \tag{3.23}$$

Compared with (2.12), we have reduced a and c in approximately the same proportion to make room for a positive "b". The long-run rate of profit from (2.12) was 8%, and would be doubled if s were halved. From (3.16) and (3.23) we now find a long-run rate of profit equal to 4.7%, and halving the saving rate only increases the rate of profit to 7.3%. From (3.22) and (3.23) we see that the value of m/n giving $\dot{v}/v=0$ is 0.42. With $g=n+m=0.04$, this means that $v(t)$ will rise as long as the growth of the labor force does not exceed 2.8%.

It is easy to see that the long-run rate of profit in the model in Section II will go to infinity as s approaches zero. This relationship does not hold for the present case; from (3.16) we see that $s=0$ gives $\pi=gc/b$. In the numerical example (3.23) this means that the rate of profit is bounded above by the value 9.6% (assuming a non-negative saving rate). The lower bound for $\bar{\pi}$ is for $s=a$, giving $\bar{\pi}=gc/(1-a)$. In our numerical example this value is 3.2%. These bounds indicate that the effect of the saving rate on the long-run rate of profit is rather limited when the economy is constrained by an exhaustible resource.

Let us now turn to the case in which $g=0$. From (3.12) and the fact that $\pi = ax$ we get

$$\frac{\dot{\pi}}{\pi} = \frac{\dot{x}}{x} = -\frac{ab+cs}{1-b}x. \qquad (3.24)$$

In other words, any positive value of s will imply that the rate of profit will always be falling, and that the rate of decline will become lower, the lower the rate of profit is. From (3.10) and (3.11) we get

$$\frac{\dot{R}}{R} = \frac{\dot{x}}{x} - (a-s)x, \qquad (3.25)$$

i.e. the resource use will decrease over time (since $s<a$). From (3.11) and (3.24) we get

$$\frac{\dot{Y}}{Y} = \frac{a(s-b)}{1-b}x, \qquad (3.26)$$

i.e. output (and the wage rate, since $w=aY/L$ and L is constant) will rise, remain constant or decline depending on whether $s>b$, $s=b$ or $s<b$. Note that if $b>a$, $a>s$ will imply that output *must* be declining. As before, the resource price will always increase by the rate π, i.e. a gradually declining rate.

Even if s drops to zero when π becomes sufficiently small, it follows from (3.24) that the rate of profit will continue to decline. For $s=0$ we see that the wage rate and output will also be declining; cf. (3.26). The only way a declining rate of profit can be prevented in this model is to have a sufficiently large *negative* saving rate. From (3.24) we see that π and x will remain constant if $s = -ab/c$. In this case π will remain constant, while capital, output and the wage rate decline by a constant rate which is lower than the rate of decline of resource use. The resource price will rise at a constant rate in this case.

IV. Concluding Comments

As mentioned in Section I, Wicksell's main objection to Cassel's view of how the rate of profit would develop was that Wicksell did not agree with the idea that no saving would take place for a sufficiently low rate of profit. However, as we just have seen, when exhaustible resources are taken into consideration, the rate of profit will continue to decline even if the saving rate should drop to zero. This fact strengthens Wicksell's argument that the main factors which prevent the rate of profit from falling are labor growth and technical progress.

When there is growth in the economy, three important conclusions follow from the preceding analysis. First, we saw that the existence of a scarce non-renewable natural resource in a sense depresses the long-run rate of profit compared with what it would be otherwise in an economy without such resource scarcity.

Our second conclusion concerns the sensitivity of the long-run rate of profit to the saving rate. The existence of a scarce non-renewable resource makes the rate of profit less sensitive to the saving rate than it is without such resource scarcity. A numerical example indicated that regardless of what the saving rate is, the long-run rate of profit will lie in a relatively small region which is independent of the saving rate.

The third and last conclusion we can draw is that the long-run rate of profit is proportional to the sum of the rates of labor growth and labor augmenting technical progress regardless of whether or not natural resource scarcity enters into our model (as long as we consider Cobb–Douglas production functions). This last conclusion supports Knut Wicksell's view that the two most important factors in determining the long-run development of the rate of profit are labor growth and technical progress.

References

Burmeister, E., Caton, C., Dobell, A. R. & Ross, S.: The 'Saddlepoint Property' and the structure of dynamic heterogeneous capital good models. *Econometrica 41*, 79–95, 1973.

Cassel, G.: *Nature and necessity of interest*. London, 1903.

Dasgupta, P. & Heal, G.: The optimal depletion of exhaustible resources. *The Review of Economic Studies*, Symposium on the Economics of Exhaustible Resources, pp. 3–28, 1974.

Dixit, A. K.: *The theory of equilibrium growth*. Oxford University Press, London, 1976.

Garg, P. & Sweeney, J. L.: Optimal growth with depletable resources. *Resources and Energy 1*; 1977.

Hoel, M.: The development of the capital return in neo-classical growth theory. In M. Hoel: *Aspects of distribution and growth in a capitalist economy*. Memorandum from the Institute of Economics, University of Oslo, April 10, pp. 1–39, 1975.

Hoel, M.: *Naturressurser og økonomisk vekst*. Memorandum from the Institute of Economics, University of Oslo, July 22, 1977.

Hotelling, H.: The economics of exhaustible resources. *The Journal of Political Economy 39*, 137–175, 1931.

Ingham, A. & Simmons, P.: Natural resources and growing population. *The Review of Economic Studies 42*, 191–206, 1975.

Solow, R. M.: Intergenerational equity and exhaustible resources. *The Review of Economic Studies*, Symposium on the Economics of Exhaustible Resources, pp. 29–45, 1974.

Stiglitz, J. E.: Growth with exhaustible resources: Efficient and optimal growth paths. *The Review of Economic Studies*, Symposium on the Economics of Exhaustible Resources, pp. 123–138, 1974a.

Stiglitz, J. E.: Growth with exhaustible natural resources: The competitive economy. *The Review of Economic Studies*, Symposium on the Economics of Exhaustible Resources, pp. 139–152, 1974b.

Weinstein, M. C. & Zeckhauser, R. J.: Use patterns for depletable and recycleable resources. *The Review of Economic Studies*, Symposium on the Economics of Exhaustible Resources, pp. 67–88, 1974.

Wicksell, K.: *Föreläsningar i nationalekonomi*, I. C. W. K. Gleerups Förlag, Lund, 1928.

WICKSELL ON THE CURRENCY THEORY VS. THE BANKING PRINCIPLE*

Trygve Haavelmo

University of Oslo, Oslo, Norway

Abstract

In his search for a positive theory of the value of money Wicksell found the Quantity Theory and, even more so, the Banking Principle, quite inadequate. It is argued in this paper that Wicksell may have underestimated the theoretical value of the Banking Principle and that this principle is not incompatible with Wicksell's own "Positive Solution".

I. Introduction

Few have had Wicksell's capacity to penetrate verbose debates in order to grasp the essentials. But in his attempt to absolve the controversy between advocates of the Currency Theory and the Banking Principle, it seems as though Wicksell himself encountered certain difficulties. The anchorman on the Currency Theory side, *Ricardo*, obviously impressed Wicksell as much as he did others with a sense of theoretical acumen. Concerning the actual basis for Ricardo's point of view, namely the Quantity Theory of money, Wicksell says: "The only specific theory of the value of money which has ever been formulated and the only one that can claim to be of real scientific importance, is the so-called Quantity Theory, ...".[1] And Ricardo's famous paper on "The High Price of Bullion", is characterized by Wicksell as "a shining pearl in the economic literature".[2]

With regard to the Banking Principle, Wicksell begins with the following, indeed not completely flattering, description: "... an unclear name for what is actually a rather unclear concept ...".[3] This is presumably addressed to *Thomas Tooke*.

---

* As the main source of references for this paper, I used Knut Wicksell, *Föreläsningar i Nationalekonomi* (Lectures in Economics), Vol. II, 3rd edition, Lund, 1929 (edited by Emil Sammarin). References to this volume in the subsequent text are indicated by the page number only. As a supplementary source, I used the English edition of Wicksell's *Geldzins und Güterpreise*, entitled *Interest and Prices*, London, 1936. I am indebted to my colleague Eivind Bjøntegård for important corrections in my original manuscript. I also want to thank Julie Sundqvist for translating my manuscript, originally in Norwegian.

[1] p. 132.
[2] p. 165.
[3] p. 161.

Wicksell's own view of the problem is clear from the very beginning. He wants to formulate a theory which can explain, in a genuinely fundamental and convincing way, changes in the absolute price level (or, in other words, in the value or purchasing power of money). The Currency Theory implies that it is changes in the quantity of money which are essential and in fact constitute the driving force. The Banking Principle, on the other hand, can be interpreted to the effect that the quantity of money plays a more passive role; it adjusts in accordance with the cash requirements created by changes in the value of transactions when the price level is forced up or down by *other* factors.

If this highly simplified description of the controversy can be accepted, it seems to me that basically, Wicksell *should have sided with the advocates of the Banking Principle*, since their viewpoint, interpreted somewhat generously, can be said to coincide with ideas in Wicksell's own "positive solution".[1] In the following, I shall try to reflect on this idea in more detail. At the same time, there is reason to emphasize that Wicksell does not present the facts in the controversy in such a simplified and rigid way as I have above. He permits the parties to express numerous subarguments and factual information so as to penetrate substantially, and expose, the thought processes of both sides. Wicksell is the patient, but stern, judge.

Below, I use some simple models. They are not formulated explicitly by Wicksell, but I believe they are quite evident from Wicksell's verbal presentation.

II. The Pure Quantity Theory

This theory can be regarded as referring to possible effects on the price level in a society, of an exogenously given increase in the quantity of money. Wicksell is dissatisfied with Hume's fiction whereby we all wake up one morning with redoubled cash holdings. Wicksell thinks it seems more reasonable to conceive of a sudden discovery of gold.[2] But as far as I understand Wicksell, one could just as well consider an increase in any other pure means of exchange, such as paper money, when this means of exchange is limited in quantity, authorized and generally accepted.

We use the following symbols, regarded as macro variables (or averages): X = volume of goods and services, P = price level, M = quantity of money, V = velocity of circulation of money, R = nominal national income. Indices, etc. will be added as the need arises.

One important simplification to be used in the following should perhaps be considered more closely from the outset. We shall assume that X is *constant*.

---

[1] pp. 177 ff.
[2] p. 150.

This may seem highly drastic in view of the essential role Wicksell assigns to the concept of investment. It means that real growth processes and real trade cycles are disregarded. The point is, however, that the present analysis is not concerned with the complex effects of factors such as these. Rather, it deals with statements about purely *monetary phenomena*. It is not some conceivable confusion between monetary and real aspects, or a lack of understanding of the relations between the two, which is the point of matters discussed here. But this of course means that *empirical* observations of the quantity of money and the price level are not directly relevant data for studying the strength of the Quantity Theory. Wicksell expressed himself quite clearly and unambigously on this point.[1]

We start from the equation of exchange,

$$PX = VM. \tag{1}$$

Then if the ratio between X and V is constant, or if both of these magnitudes are constant, we obtain the Quantity Theory in its static, but indisputable and almost banal form: It is impossible for P and M to move in any way other than proportionally.

A constant velocity, V, raises a question which is not entirely trivial concerning *invariance* in relation to changes in the unit of measurement of *time*. If V denotes the number of "rotations" per year, then the number of rotations per month would only be one-twelfth as large. But here there is a pitfall which, indirectly, has been revealed by those who maintain that the Quantity Theory has hardly any special importance or relevance for a stationary economy with everything wholly foreseeable. The point is that a transaction demand for money must be assumed to be linked to some kind of *horizon* for expected transactions. Clearly, the chance of becoming illiquid is not as great for a month as for a year. Assume that the value of the total of transactions PX is reckoned "per year". Let the "horizon" be h. The transaction equation should then be written: volume of transactions per year multiplied by the horizon h (in years) = the average number of rotations of a unit of money *per h* multiplied by the quantity of money. A constant V then means that the number of rotations *per h* is constant. If we then decide, for example, to calculate the value of transactions PX per month, this figure will be only $1/12$ of the number per year, while at the same time h will be 12 times larger, so that the Quantity Theory becomes meaningful with a constant V, regardless of the unit of measurement of time.

Here and in the subsequent analysis, we presuppose for the sake of simplicity that h is so large that it is reasonable to assume $V > 1$. This also implies that later on, when we let $t = 0, 1, 2, \ldots$, this actually means $t = 0, h, 2h, \ldots$ The question of a fixed value of h, in years or months, is complicated, both theoretically and econometrically. (Wicksell concerns himself a great deal with the

---

[1] pp. 135–136.

concept of velocity, but his line of thinking is not so easily understood; cf. *Interest and Prices*, pp. 51–80.)

The Quantity Theory can be given a somewhat artificial, dynamic form. Assume that the relation between national income, R, and the value of transactions, PX, is *constant* and that, for simplicity, the ratio is 1. (The latter can be obtained through suitable manipulations of units of measurement.) We then have

$$R = PX. \tag{2}$$

Let us consider a discrete process and let the index t denote point in time, t. Assume that at time $t=0$, an additional ΔM_0 of money becomes available to the public. The point is that this has to be regarded as *income*. (How should it otherwise be entered into the books, in an economy without credit?) X and V are assumed *constant*. Then if M_t and P_t denote the variables which at any point in time satisfy (1), we could conceive of the following process:

$$R_{t+1} = R_t + (M_0 + \Delta M_0 - M_t) \tag{3}$$

$$M_t = \frac{R_t}{V} = P_t \frac{X}{V}. \tag{4}$$

The difference in the right-hand side of (3) is thus the share of the total volume of money which the public does not require as cash at time t, and which it, therefore, tries to use up for the only alternative available, that is, for the purchase of goods and services.

Incidentally, equation (3) illustrates that dimensional analysis in economics is sometimes tricky. The equation may give the impression that we are adding together stocks and flows which, of course, would be absurd. The point is that in front of the second term to the right in (3) there is a coefficient which has the dimension "part of, per unit of t". This coefficient is not visible because we have assumed that it is equal to 1. The same applies to equation (10) below.

From (3) and (4) we obtain

$$R_{t+1} = \left(1 - \frac{1}{V}\right) R_t + M_0 + \Delta M_0 \tag{5}$$

$$M_{t+1} = \left(1 - \frac{1}{V}\right) M_t + \frac{M_0 + \Delta M_0}{V} \tag{6}$$

$$P_{t+1} = \left(1 - \frac{1}{V}\right) P_t + \frac{M_0 + \Delta M_0}{X}. \tag{7}$$

The stability requirement $V > \frac{1}{2}$ is already met by our previous simplifying assumption that $V > 1$. Stable, stationary solutions are then, obviously

$$\bar{R} = V(M_0 + \Delta M_0), \bar{M} = M_0 + \Delta M_0, \bar{P} = \frac{V}{X}(M_0 + \Delta M_0),$$

which agrees with the static Quantity Theory.

For the sake of completeness, let us add the following. Assume that $\Delta M_0 = 0$. Then, in this model, it would be completely meaningless to ask "what would happen if the price level rose". Thus, the Banking Principle is irrelevant here. In fact, it would seem rather preposterous to connect the Banking Principle with an economy without credit. But the model may perhaps serve to support Wicksell's criticism of Ricardo with regard to explaining explicitly how new money enters into circulation.[1]

III. An Economy with Banks and Borrowing Possibilities

Let us now consider an economy which, for simplicity, consists of two sectors, a *banking system* and the *public*. In order for the public to come into possession of a larger quantity of money (we disregard counterfeiting, etc.), two different possibilities are conceivable: (1) the banking system can, in one way or another, *give* the public money as a gift, or (2) the public can *borrow* from the banking system. (Possible interest charges can be seen as returned to the public in the form of profits, so that the banking system will have no net income.) In the first case, transactions are related to the public's *income account* and in the second case to its *balance account*.

Let M_t be the public's chosen cash in hand at any time and let L_t be its net borrowing in the banking system. All money is assumed to come from the banking system. Assume that at the outset, all money, M_0, is *borrowed in the banking system*. We then have

$$M_0 = L_0. \tag{8}$$

We assume that the public's initial position is in equilibrium, that is

$$P_0 X = V M_0. \tag{9}$$

(X and V are still assumed *constant*.)

Assume now that at time $t=0$, the banking system *gives* the public an amount of cash $=\Delta M_0$. This would be an *increase in income* for the public. Assume that, at $t=1$, this amount is used (or is attempted to be used) to purchase more goods and services. We then get

$$P_1 X = P_0 X + \Delta M_0. \tag{10}$$

How much cash is required to cover these transactions? Obviously

$$M_1 = \frac{X}{V} P_1 = M_0 + \frac{\Delta M_0}{V}. \tag{11}$$

The remainder is paid off on loans in the banking system, that is

$$L_1 = L_0 - \left(1 - \frac{1}{V}\right) \Delta M_0. \tag{12}$$

---

[1] Cf. pp. 166–167.

This puts a stop to any further increases in the price level. (The possible effect of wealth on demand is a complex problem and will not be discussed here.) Then the advocates of the Banking Principle are correct in their view that superfluous cash flows back to the banks. They are also right when they claim that the primary element in this process is not that ΔM_0 takes the form of cash but that it means an *increase in demand*. A nominal increase in income could in fact be produced by people themselves by bidding up prices for each other (a moderate temporary increase in V) and by borrowing from the banking system so as to cover the increased cash requirements. Wicksell's own "positive solution" of course lies in showing that the public's excess demand is the primary force, which also inflates the value of PX, owing to expected profits when *the interest rate is too low in relation to expected capital earnings*. (It goes without saying that Wicksell dealt with his famous "cumulative process" much more explicitly and in greater detail than is indicated here.)

Let us now consider the case where the banking system does not hand out any such doles as assumed above. Clearly then, the left and right-hand sides in the equation

$$L_t = M_t \tag{13}$$

move along passively in order to cover the public's cash requirements, which in turn depend on $P_t X$. As far as I can see, this agrees well with the fundamental idea of the Banking Principle.

There are two reasons why Wicksell does not seem to be very enthusiastic about the Banking Principle. First, there are many unclear details which must have been annoying to Wicksell's brilliant theoretical mind. Second, and in particular, advocates of the Banking Principle to some extent avoided what Wicksell regarded as the essential problem, i.e. the question of what causes price to move. In any case, I feel that some of Tooke's ideas actually must have found some positive response with Wicksell.[1]

IV. Interest Rates and Velocity of Circulation

Wicksell dealt extensively with the concept of the velocity of circulation of money and its effects on price development, with references to both the Quantity Theory and to the question of the transactions demand for money in general.[2] In this context, we shall treat only one side of the matter, which seems important with regard to attempts of both the Currency Theory and the Banking Principle to unite theory and practical experience, and Wicksell's own efforts to understand certain observed covariations between prices, the volume of money and interest rates.[3]

---

[1] Cf. p. 170.
[2] Cf. pp. 157 ff.
[3] Cf. especially p. 186 and pp. 189–191.

A reasonable version of what is today known as liquidity theory seems to be that the velocity, V, is a function of the rate of interest. Let us designate the latter r_t. We then assume that

$$V_t = V(r_t), \tag{14}$$

where higher interest rates imply a higher V, and vice versa. If a high velocity is inconvenient for the public, why should the banking system bother the public with it unnecessarily? Why not maintain a low interest rate, perhaps equal to 0? Wicksell asks this question himself,[1] but he clears up the muddle. There are *other* reasons why this kind of interest rate policy cannot be carried out. Interest rates have a *double function*. The other is to influence the demand for real capital, when potential borrowers compare the prospects of returns with necessary interest expenditures.

Let $\bar{r}_t$ denote the prospects of the rate of return (Wicksell's "normal rate of interest"). We can then represent Wicksell's theory on this point as

$$\dot{R}_t = \frac{d(P_t X)}{dt} = f(\bar{r}_t - r_t), \tag{15}$$

where the relation between $\dot{R}$ and $(\bar{r}_t - r_t)$ is positive. If X is still constant, then P_t *increases* as long as $(\bar{r}_t - r_t)$ is positive. What does this imply with respect to the relation over time between prices, the volume of money and interest rates? The public's equation for liquidity balance can now be written

$$L_t = \frac{P_t X}{V(r_t)} = M_t \tag{16}$$

that is, by differentiating and inserting (15),

$$\dot{M}_t = X \frac{\dot{P}_t V(r_t) - P_t V'(r_t) \dot{r}_t}{(V(r_t))^2} = \frac{f(\bar{r}_t - r_t)}{V(r_t)} - M_t \frac{V'(r_t)}{V(r_t)} \dot{r}_t \tag{16a}$$

Equation (15) indicates that as long as $(\bar{r}_t - r_t)$ is positive, prices rise. But the question as to whether the volume of money, M_t, will increase depends on which of the two terms on the right-hand side of (16a) is largest. This makes it easy to see that the observed relation between the price level and the quantity of money can be complex and that Wicksell's concern for both the Currency Theory and the Banking Principle on this point was well founded.

---

[1] Cf. p. 181.

THE LONG-RUN DEMAND FOR MONEY—
A WICKSELLIAN APPROACH*

Lars Jonung

University of Lund, Lund, Sweden

Abstract

The income velocity of money in several countries such as Sweden, the United States and Great Britain, displays a U-shaped pattern for the last one hundred years. This paper proposes an explanation of this secular behavior based on an extension of Wicksell's work on velocity emphasizing the influence of institutional changes. The secular fall in velocity in the last half of the 19th century and the first part of the 20th century is regarded as the outcome of a process of monetization encompassing (1) a growing use of money at the expense of a decline in barter and payment in kind, and (2) an increase in the activity of commercial banks with respect to supplying notes and bank deposits to the public. The secular rise in velocity is viewed as the result of two developments, increasing financial sophistication and growing economic security and stability. The explanation suggested here is confronted with some relevant empirical evidence. The paper, being exploratory in character, deals primarily with the Swedish record.

> "Theoretically, therefore, the concept of velocity of circulation is a very simple one. But in practice its investigation is one of the most difficult problems in economics", K. Wicksell, *Lectures II*, p. 60.

I. Introduction

As a result of the restatement of the quantity theory of money, the determinants of the demand for money have been the subject of considerable research. Much of recent econometric work on the demand for money has been based on the view that real income, sometimes regarded as a proxy for wealth, and interest rates are the major explanatory variables for the long-run behavior of velocity. This paper stresses a different set of explanatory variables, sug-

---

* This paper has benefited greatly from the suggestions of Michael Bordo of Carleton University. I also wish to acknowledge the helpful comments of the participants at the workshop in monetary economics at UCLA; Don Patinkin, Anna Schwartz, Arne Jon Isachsen; and colleagues at the Departments of Economics and Economic History at the University of Lund. Mark Olson has improved my English.

This paper is part of a joint project carried out by the author and M. Bordo, aimed at studying the long-run behavior of velocity across a number of countries.

gesting that other factors than those given such prominence in recent studies of the demand for money, have exerted a primary influence on the secular movements of velocity. A hypothesis is put forth here emphasizing the role of certain institutional changes. These institutional developments are associated with changes in the relative returns of holding money and other assets, inducing a series of substitutions between various assets performing monetary and non-monetary services. Thus the secular swings in velocity are viewed as the outcome of such substitutions. The explanation advanced should be regarded as an extension and development of Knut Wicksell's analysis of changes in velocity.

This article is organized as follows. First, data on the long-run movements of velocity between the 1870's and 1970's are presented. Second, Knut Wicksell's theory of changes in velocity is surveyed. Next, this analysis is extended upon to account for the secular pattern of velocity previously described. The extended Wicksellian hypothesis suggested here is then confronted with some empirical evidence bearing on it. Finally, some comparisons are made to other explanations of the secular movements in velocity. The discussion in this article is primarily based on the Swedish experience, but references are also made to the American and British records.

II. The Empirical Picture

The secular behavior of the income velocity of money in Sweden for the period 1871–1971 is displayed in Chart 1. This chart shows two velocity curves. The first curve exhibits the annual ratios of the nominal income to the money stock. This ratio falls from a level of around 6 in the early 1870's to a low of around 1.5 in the early 1920's. Then it starts on an upward trend, reaching a level of slightly above 3 in the 1960's. Thus velocity describes a U-shaped secular pattern. It also displays a cyclical behavior as seen from the short-run fluctuations around the long-run trend. These cyclical swings are smoothed out by the second velocity curve in order to bring out the U-formed pattern more clearly.

In Chart 1 the money stock is defined as the holdings by the public of notes and demand and time deposits with the commercial banking system, that is an M_2-definition is employed. The use of other definitions of the money stock—an M_1-concept excluding the time deposits with the commercial banks or an M_3-aggregate including the deposits with the savings bank system—does not alter the general shape of the secular velocity curve of Sweden.

The long-run movements in the income velocity of money for the United States and Great Britain also exhibit a U-shaped pattern. Velocity fell in the United States from 5 in 1880 to a low of approximately 1.5 in the late 1940's. Velocity was falling in Great Britain during the same time period as in the United States, although the decline is less pronounced. The British velocity

Chart 1. The Income Velocity of Money in Sweden, 1871–1971. The dotted line connects the annual observations. The solid line displays the velocity curve smoothed by a spline function to bring out the secular pattern.

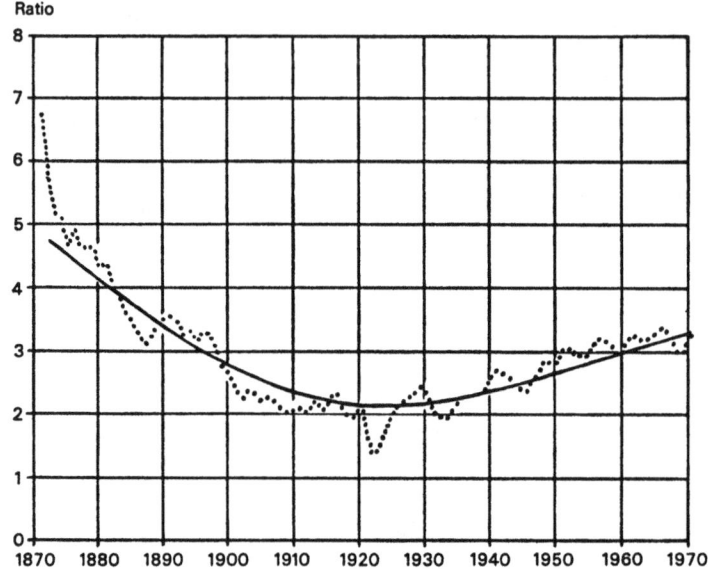

Comments: The money stock is defined as public holdings of notes and demand and time deposits with the commercial banks computed as annual averages of end-of-month figures. Other definitions of the money stock also give rise to a U-shaped curve. Due to restrictions on the computer program, the observation for 1871 is excluded from the calculations of the smoothed curve.

Sources: Nominal income is taken from Ö. Johansson, *The Gross Domestic Product of Sweden and its Composition, 1861–1955*, Stockholm, 1967, linked to national income statistics from the Central Bureau of Statistics for the period 1956–1971.

was slightly above 2 in the 1880's. The dating of the turning points is the same in Britain as in the United States. Since the late 1940's velocity has been rising in both countries.[1]

Available evidence on the long-run behavior of velocity for a number of other countries generally confirms a similar U-shaped pattern of velocity as in Sweden, the United States and Great Britain. This seems at least to be the case for the following countries—Australia, Canada, Denmark, Finland, Germany and Norway.[2]

III. Wicksell on Changes in the Transactions Velocity of Hard Cash

The analysis of velocity occupies a central position in Wicksell's monetary theory. He treats extensively the determinants of velocity in *Interest and*

---
[1] See Figure 1, p. 139 in Schwartz (1975).
[2] Consistent time series on velocity for these countries are presented in a forthcoming study by Bordo & Jonung.

Prices as well as in the *Lectures*.[1] His analysis of velocity revolves around the development of credit as a substitute for "money"—"money" being defined by him as "hard cash", that is, as equal to metallic currency or gold. Bank notes and bank deposits are thus not regarded as "money" but as close substitutes for hard cash. The growth of such assets as well as of other types of credit will influence the velocity of hard cash. In Wicksell's words:[2]

> the influence of credit on currency, may, *under all circumstances*, be regarded as accelerating the circulation of money ... The occasions on which credit actually replaces money ... may, quite simply, be regarded as special cases of the general acceleration of circulation; for instead of a purely physical transfer of money we have a *virtual*, i.e. a merely imaginary or possible transfer, but of the same effectiveness.

Thus, the growth of substitutes for metallic currency, implies that a given amount of hard cash can form the basis for a larger volume of transactions than previously was the case. As a consequence of this expansion of money substitutes, virtual velocity will increase.

This argument may be summarized in the following manner. Let T denote the volume of transactions per period and G the amount of metallic currency held by the non-bank public, where G is equivalent to Wicksell's definition of money. The ratio of T to G then represents the transactions velocity of money according to Wicksell.

(1) $V_g = \dfrac{T}{G}$ the transactions velocity of hard cash ($=$ gold).

In a pure cash economy with no credit and no banks, actual velocity will be equal to the physical velocity of the metallic money in use, as every transaction is settled with hard cash. When credit in the form of bank notes and bank deposits is introduced, this picture will change. Let D represent the amount of bank notes and deposits used as means of payment, then the transactions velocity of the sum of notes and deposits can be expressed in the following way:

(2) $V_d = \left(\dfrac{T}{G}\right) \cdot \left(\dfrac{G}{D}\right)$ the transactions velocity of notes and deposits.

that is, as the product of the transactions velocity of hard cash, and the ratio of hard cash to notes and deposits. The introduction of notes and deposits replacing gold in transactions will cause a rise in virtual velocity ($=T/G$), assuming that the replaced gold is taken over by the banks.[3] In the extreme case

---

[1] See Chapter 6 in *Interest and Prices* and Part III in *Lectures II*. Wicksell also discusses changes in velocity in a number of other places, notably in a speech at the annual meeting of the *Bankmannaförening* (the Association of the Employees of the Commercial Banks) in 1902. Here Wicksell (1902) deals more explicitly with the Swedish monetary situation, explaining how the spread of bank notes in Sweden had increased virtual velocity.
[2] *Lectures II*, p. 67.
[3] Generally speaking, a more rapid growth in the volume of transactions (T) than in the amount of gold held by the public (G) raises virtual velocity. Thus, Wicksell's argument

the public holds no gold and only uses bank money which makes virtual velocity equal to infinity. This is the case of Wicksell's "pure credit system"—the polar case of the pure cash economy—where the public has no monetary use of gold.

Wicksell discusses in detail the effects of various institutional arrangements for granting credit on virtual velocity. Credit given between private individuals without the intervention of financial intermediaries, that is "simple credit",[1] has only a very limited influence as a substitute for money tending to accelerate the velocity of circulation.

The appearance of "organized credit", specifically in the form of commercial banking, will have far-reaching effects, however. The major part of Wicksell's analysis of velocity actually deals with the growth of banks, which he regards as "the heart and centre of modern currency systems".[2]

Through the development of banking, gold is gradually replaced by bank credit, that is, by notes and deposits. Wicksell envisages a system where all gold eventually ends up in the vaults of the banking system as reserves.[3] He argues that the reserve-deposit ratio of the banking system will decline over time as the result of two factors. First, "the law of large numbers", and second, transactions between customers of the same bank will be settled through book-keeping transfers from one account to another, reducing the demand for gold as reserves by the banks. Returning to Expression (2), this means that the ratio of G to D can be regarded as the reserve ratio of the banking system. Wicksell expects this ratio to approach zero over time, hoping that gold will lose all its monetary use in the future. Then the "ideal" banking system would operate without any metallic currency and virtual velocity would be infinitely large.

Wicksell's major argument is that the gradual replacement of gold by bank notes and bank deposits will raise the virtual velocity of hard cash. Thus, the

---

is consistent with a growing volume of gold in the hands of the public as long as the volume of transactions is expanding at a faster rate, presumably due to the use of bank money for settling transactions to a larger extent than previously. However, the tenor of Wicksell's analysis of virtual velocity suggests that he envisaged an actual decline in the volume of gold held by the non-bank public. See Part III in *Lectures*.

[1] Ibid., p. 70.
[2] Ibid., p. 73.
[3] Ibid., p. 84.
[4] Ibid., p. 85. Wicksell points to a number of obstacles to the realization of the "ideal bank" but he hopes that they will be eliminated in the future. According to him the demonetization of gold through the replacement of bank-produced monies "would undoubtedly be a very great national saving"; *Lectures II*, p. 123. Wicksell's discussion here may be compared with the present-day analysis of inside–outside money. Gold represents outside money and bank notes and bank deposits inside money. The progressive substitution of inside money for outside money—which is the essence of Wicksell's theory of velocity—represents a gain for society as a whole. Resources previously used for the production of gold for monetary use may now be released for other purposes. Cf. Johnson (1969). The demonetization of gold is actually a necessary condition for a central bank to adopt Wicksell's norm of price stabilization, as this norm requires that the central bank is able to control the domestic money stock.

growth of commercial banking is the central theme of his analysis. He also points out some other institutional developments that will influence the public's holdings of currency, notes and deposits. He argues that the transition from a barter economy to a monetary economy will increase the demand for currency and for bank-produced means of payment.[1] Furthermore, when discussing the problem of empirically testing the quantity theory, he states that "commercial progress" will induce a more efficient use of existing media of exchange, that is, he is implying that technological and financial innovations may influence the velocity of notes and deposits.[2]

IV. A Suggested Extension of Wicksell's Approach

Wicksell analyzed the rise in the transactions velocity of metallic currency, dealing specifically with gold. His approach can be developed into a hypothesis which accounts for the long-run behavior of velocity as displayed in Chart 1, that is, one which explains the income velocity of money, where the money stock is defined as the holdings by the public of notes and commercial bank deposits. Judging from the chart there are two movements in velocity to be explained: first, the long-run fall, and second, the subsequent secular rise. It seems reasonable to begin by analyzing the factors causing the downward trend and then to examine the developments behind the secular rise. The horizontal section of the velocity curve would then mark a transition period, when the forces causing the downward trend were roughly counterbalanced by the developments causing an upward trend. (From here on "velocity" stands for the income velocity of money where the money stock encompasses notes and total commercial bank deposits held by the public.)

(i) *Monetization and the Secular Fall of Velocity*

The downward trend in velocity may be explained by a monetization process. This process consists of two closely interrelated developments: (1) a growing use of "money" for settling transactions at the expense of a decline in barter and a payment in kind, occurring simultaneously with an expansion of markets and decline of production for own consumption;[3] and (2) the rise of commercial banks supplying the public with notes and deposit facilities. It should be expected that these two developments—representing the monetization of the economy—would during one period of economic development cause a more

---

[1] *Lectures II*, pp. 66 and 145.
[2] Ibid., p. 145.
[3] Montgomery (1939, p. 59) describes this development in the Swedish agricultural sector as "commercialization" meaning that "production for the market superseded, to an ever-growing extent, the ancient rural economy where the peasant households, or the villages, had been largely self-supporting units". The process of "commercialization" started in Sweden in the middle of the 19th century according to Montgomery.

rapid growth in the demand for money than in nominal income and dominate over other secular influences on velocity.[1]

(ii) *Financial Sophistication, Growing Security and Stability, and the Secular Rise of Velocity*

The upward trend in velocity may be explained by two major developments: (1) an increasing financial sophistication, and (2) a growing economic security and stability. "Financial sophistication" describes two trends; first, the appearance of a large number of close substitutes for money such as bonds, stocks and other financial assets; and second, the development of various methods of economizing on money balances, such as the use of credit cards, transfer of funds electronically or by phone, and modern cash management techniques within business and industry.[2]

In a modern welfare state the individual is guaranteed—predominantly through provisions made by the public sector—a certain minimum standard in case of unemployment, disease, or retirement. He is often spared the expenses of child birth, costs of education and other costs associated with the rearing of children. Health and dental care are also provided at low or nominal fees. Stabilization policies in the post-war period have generally been geared towards maintaining full employment and minimizing fluctuations in the business cycle. These developments, which may be grouped under the heading of "growing security and stability", reduce the returns of holding money as precautionary reserves and as a store of value.[3] In summary, financial sophistication and growing stability and security are suggested to be decisive factors behind the long-run rise in velocity that can be observed in a large number of countries.

---

[1] The methods adopted in the construction of national income data are of importance in the analysis of the effects of monetization on the income velocity of money. Ideally only final income transactions settled with money should be included in the numerator of velocity. Chart 1 is based on income series with relatively few imputations for the 19th century, thus the non-monetary elements are kept at a minimum.

[2] Due to e.g. technological developments within the banking sector, the flow of monetary services of a given amount of real money holdings has increased over time. Klein (1977) shows in a theoretical analysis that the net effect on the demand for money of technological developments is ambiguous, ignoring real income effects. This study suggests, however, that technological changes have contributed to a rising secular velocity.

[3] The system of taxation in modern economies, accompanying the growth of the public sector, may strongly reduce the returns of holding money, except in the form of notes. In Sweden a comprehensive tax system covering almost all market transactions as well as income from interest payments on deposits has decreased the demand for money for settling transactions as well as for storing wealth, contributing e.g., to tendencies of a return to barter, that is to a process of demonetization. All factors that induce demonetization contribute to a rising velocity. This is the case with vertical integration. The rise of a large public sector also raises questions concerning the definition of income to be employed in the calculations of velocity; see Selden (1956, pp. 242–43). These questions are not considered here as data are not readily available on the non-monetary elements of the share of national income contributed by the public sector. The national income data used in Chart 1 include the public sector. A proper exclusion of the non-monetary elements would lower the level of velocity for the 1950's and 1960's but the secular rise will remain significant, judging from the size of the contribution of the public sector to the Swedish national income.

The hypothesis proposed here is based on the concept of substitution. First, there is a substitution into money in the form of notes and deposits replacing other arrangements for payments and for storing wealth. Second, new substitutes for money develop over time inducing portfolio holders to switch out of money into the new assets. Thus, the process of monetization as well as that of financial sophistication and of growing security and stability gives rise to a chain of substitutions. At a certain stage of economic development the monetization process dominates over other influences causing a falling velocity. At a later stage the appearance of various substitutes for money contributes to a rising ratio of income to money. The relative strengths of these two forces determine the dating of the turning point of velocity.

The explanation suggested above consists of two parts; the first one dealing with the secular fall of velocity, the second one with the secular rise of velocity. Wicksell focused upon the transition from metallic currency and barter to bank monies when he discusses the rise in the transactions velocity of metallic currency. The extended Wicksellian approach includes this process of monetization to account for the fall of the income velocity of money (defined as notes and deposits), but it also incorporates the appearance of substitutes for bank monies such as bonds, stocks and social security provisions and government compensation schemes to explain the subsequent rise of velocity. Thus the extended Wicksellian approach deals with a later phase in the development of the monetary system than that discussed by Wicksell as well as with the earlier monetization process. It should be stressed that both Wicksell's discussion of the transactions velocity of metallic currency and the extended Wicksellian hypothesis dealing with the income velocity of notes and bank deposits put great emphasis on institutional changes.

V. The Empirical Evidence

The hypothesis presented here stresses the importance of examining the role of institutional developments over long periods of time to account for the secular behavior of velocity. An econometric test of this hypothesis encounters considerable problems as the relevant institutional factors are generally difficult to quantify, for example rising expectations of stability and security do not easily lend themselves to any single all-inclusive measure. Furthermore, lack of consistent data for long stretches of time is another obstacle. Still, a brief overview of some indicators and evidence concerning the proposed hypothesis will be presented here. These indicators may then serve as proxy variables in econometric studies. The discussion below deals primarily with the Swedish record.

(i) *Measures of Monetization*
It is generally agreed that barter was gradually replaced by monetary ex-

change during the process of industrialization. Various accounts of payment practices describe this process in qualitative terms. A number of indicators or proxy variables for the monetization of the economy can be suggested. The following variables are of interest when studying the Swedish experience. Others may also be proposed.

Changes in the composition of the money stock. The monetization process can be retraced by studying the composition of the money stock. At the early stages of commercial banking, banks were primarily suppling notes that were used as a medium of exchange replacing specie and barter. Actually, the first Swedish commercial banks were reluctant to accept deposits. Later, the volume of demand and time deposits started to expand at a rate faster than the note issue. Thus, the currency–money ratio—that is, the ratio of notes to the total money stock—can be used as a measure of the monetization process, at least prior to the 1930's.[1] In Sweden, this ratio fell from a level around 30 per cent in the 1870's to a level around 12 per cent in the 1920's. Data on this ratio for other countries suggest a similar trend.[2]

The number of persons per bank office. The number of persons per bank office is a good indicator of the spread of commercial banking and thus of the monetization of the economy. In Sweden this number declined from 30 000 persons in 1871 to around 4 500 persons in 1922, that is, it reached a low at the same time as velocity reached its turning point. See Chart 1. However, the number of persons per bank office does not exhibit a consistent upward trend after the 1920's.

Other measures. Several accounts of changes in payment practices and transaction arrangements indicate a growing use of money at the expense of barter and payment in kind during the last half of the 19th century. One measure of this development is the share of the total wage bill represented by payments in kind. For example, at the *Söderfors* ironworks in central Sweden, the ratio of benefits in kind to total annual earnings of the workers fell from 26 per cent in 1860 to 10 per cent in 1885 and to about one per cent in 1905 as an average for year-round workers. It is difficult, however, to find data on this ratio covering the whole labor force, as payment practices varied considerably among occupations and regions, ignoring the problem of estimating the benefits in kind in monetary units. Assuming that the use of money was fostered by expanding urbanization and industrial growth, changes in the composition of the labor force and in the distribution of the population between rural and urban areas may also be adopted as indicators.[3]

---

[1] In the 1930's and 1940's the currency ratio was rising in Sweden. This pattern is, however, explained by other factors than monetization, *i.a.* by the Depression and the Second World War.

[2] The Wicksellian hypothesis stressing the development of substitutes for prevailing types of monies suggests that the income velocity of notes should reach a low prior to the income velocity of deposits.

[3] A description of the monetization process in Sweden and various measures of monetization is found in Jonung (1976).

(ii) Measures of Financial Sophistication, and of Security and Stability

It is common knowledge that a country's financial structure becomes more well-developed during the process of economic growth. There are considerable difficulties, however, in finding suitable measures of the degree of financial sophistication for Sweden.[1] A major reason for this is the lack of comprehensive statistics on the composition of national wealth. Still a few indicators may be suggested, such as the ratio of the holdings within Sweden of government securities outside of the commercial banks and the central bank to national income. This ratio rose from 3 per cent in 1871 to about 10 per cent in 1971 reflecting the appearance of a domestic capital market and of financial institutions other than the commercial banks. It is worth noting that in the 1870's roughly 80 per cent of the Swedish national debt was in foreign hands.[2] In the 1960's this picture was changed completely as all the debt was held inside Sweden. Much suggests that there was a very rapid expansion of the domestic capital market during World War I and during the 1920's, when Sweden turned from being a net foreign borrower to a net foreign lender. This development is consistent with the dating of the turning point of velocity in the early 1920's. The sum of the assets of the insurance companies, the insurance funds, the mortgage institutions and various non-bank financial intermediaries as a share of national income may also be employed as a measure of financial development.

A good measure of growing security and stability is not easily constructed. The share of government transfers to the national income—which has increased secularly—may be a rough proxy for the security provided by the public sector. Economic stability can be represented by various time series of the fluctuations in unemployment, real income and industrial production.

In summary, various indicators can be used in order to quantify these institutional changes that are the explanatory variables of the secular behavior of velocity according to the Wicksellian hypothesis, thus facilitating empirical tests of the hypothesis. The time series briefly reviewed here generally move in a way consistent with the proposed explanations.

---

[1] Goldsmith (1955, pp. 158–159) explores various measures of the stage of financial development to employ in quantitative comparisons of financial structures. He draws two conclusions that are of interest for this study. First, he shows that financial sophistication in a number of advanced Western economies has increased secularly since the Industrial Revolution. Second, the relative share of commercial banks of the national assets has generally declined implying that a given volume of the money stock can "support a larger financial superstructure". These findings are consistent with the argument emphasizing financial sophistication as a determinant of the secular rise in the income velocity of notes and deposits.

[2] See Table III in *Betänkande angående statens och kommunernas skuldsättning* (A Report on the Debt of the Government and the Local Authorities), Stockholm, 1914. This report shows the total volume of government debt held within Sweden. As the *Riksbank* and the commercial banks held hardly any government securities, this figure is taken to represent the holdings of government securities outside of the commercial banking system and the central bank. Data for 1971 are taken from the Annual Report of the National Debt Office excluding the holdings of the *Riksbank* and the commercial banks.

(iii) *Some Evidence from Cross-Section Studies*

The explanation presented here suggests that data from cross-section studies on the levels of velocity of countries at different levels of economic growth should show the following pattern: The average velocity should first fall with a rising real income per capita, real income being a proxy for economic development. At some level of income, however, it will reach a low and then start rising again. Thus, the U-shaped pattern of Chart 1 should be born out by cross-section studies. Such a pattern has actually been reported.[1]

Specific discrepencies in the long-run pattern of velocity between different countries may also be explained by the factors stressed in the Wicksellian hypothesis. For example, the rise in velocity started earlier in Sweden than in the United States and Great Britain. The greater stability of the Swedish economy may help explain the earlier turning point in Sweden than in the US and the UK. Sweden did not take part in either World War I or World War II and the depression of the 1930's was deeper and longer lasting in the United States and Great Britain. The degree of financial development may also explain dissimilarities in the velocity trends of different countries. Friedman and Schwartz report that the US income velocity fell from a level of 5 to a level of about 2 between 1880 and 1906, while the British velocity remained roughly constant at a level of about 2 during the same interval. They rationalize this pattern by arguing that the British economy was initially more financially developed than the American but that the more rapid spread of financial institutions in America left the two economies at about equal levels of financial sophistication by 1906.[2]

VI. Some Econometric Evidence on the Secular Behavior of Velocity

In modern econometric studies of velocity, real income and interest rates are, as a rule, viewed as the main explanatory variables behind the secular fluctuations in velocity. Friedman & Schwartz have argued strongly for the existence of a secular relationship between real income and velocity in their study of the monetary history of the United States.[3] According to them money is a luxury good, that is, the demand for money rises faster than the growth in real income. Consequently, velocity is expected to fall secularly as real income rises. They base their proposition on the behavior of the US income velocity, which was falling between 1880 and 1946.

A major objection to this explanation is that it is simply inconsistent with empirical evidence. Velocity has been rising for a long time in the United

---

[1] See Anderson (1977), who reports from a 55-country income-velocity comparison, and Ezekiel & Adelkunle (1969).
[2] Schwartz (1975).
[3] Friedman & Schwartz (1963).

States and Great Britain as well as in Sweden. Friedman & Schwartz attempt to explain the post-World War II rise in velocity by stressing the effects of some special factors, primarily the rising stability of the American economy. Once the influence of these factors disappears, the secular decline is postulated to continue. Another objection to the real income hypothesis is that it does not adress the question of why the demand for money should rise faster than real income, except by definition.[1] There is an inherent risk in this approach that developments such as those emphasized in this paper are ignored. Econometric studies may then establish a relationship between real income and the demand for money which is spurious in the sense that real income and the "true" variable have followed the same trend.

Generally the demand for money is regarded as a function of interest rates, measured as the return on bonds or on some other close substitute for money, where the rate of interest represents the alternative cost of holding money. The early work of Latané in the 1950's stressed interest rates as a main determinant of velocity in the long-run.[2] Several empirical studies since then have concluded that interest rates have played a predominant role in determining velocity.[3] However, the long run movements in velocity in Sweden as surveyed here appear to be weakly related to fluctuations in interest rates. The fall in velocity took place during periods of rising as well as of falling rates. This also holds for the rise in velocity. The long-run movements in interest rates in Sweden, the United States and Great Britain are closely associated with periods of secular inflation and deflation. Consequently, one should expect velocity to fall during periods of inflation and to rise during periods of deflation. Such a consistent pattern cannot be discerned from the evidence from Sweden, the United States and Great Britain.

Interest rates also enter in the inventory approach to the theory of the demand for money, stemming from the work by Baumol and Tobin.[4] This approach assumes that there is a trade-off between two costs, the interest payment forgone by holding non-interest bearing money and the transaction costs of making exchanges between money and interest-bearing assets. Several studies have elaborated on this basic element. As a rule this class of models implies economies-of-scale in the holding of money, that is, the money demand elasticity with respect to income is less than one; in the original Baumol version it is equal to one half. Thus, these models predict a secularly rising

---

[1] See e.g. Klein (1974), Meltzer (1963) and Tobin (1965) for comments on the luxury goods hypothesis. Wicksell considers the real income elasticity of the demand for money (= metallic currency) in a discussion of the French money holding habits. "Whether a higher standard of living would itself create a tendency to maintain larger cash reserves is quite another matter. This Helfferich maintains to be true of France ... To a certain extent this may be the case, but it is probable that we are here concerned with some national pecularity, ..." *Lectures II*, pp. 66. Apparently Wicksell dismisses this version of the luxury goods hypothesis.
[2] Latané (1954) and (1960).
[3] See e.g. Klein (1974) and Meltzer (1963).
[4] Baumol (1952) and Tobin (1956).

trend of velocity. Empirical work on an aggregate level employing the inventory approach has, however, not come up with any conclusive evidence in favor of it.[1]

Various reasons may explain why econometric tests have concluded that real income and interest rates are central determinants of velocity. First, the institutional changes stressed here are difficult to quantify for long periods of time. Second, movements in real income and interest rates have covaried to a considerable extent with the explanatory variables suggested by the Wicksellian approach. Third, most money demand studies have covered fairly short periods compared to the one hundred year span discussed here. It seems plausible that the factors explaining cyclical changes in the demand for money are different from those accounting for the long-term movements in velocity.

This study stresses monetization, financial sophistication, and growing stability and security as the major explanatory variables behind the secular swings in velocity. Still, the Wicksellian approach does not exclude an influence from other variables such as those given prominence in recent econometric work. It should also be stressed that other studies—generally of a non-econometric character—have paid attention to the explanatory variables of the Wicksellian approach. However, none has given them such a central position as they are given here, nor has the work of Wicksell on velocity been acknowledged. Fisher for example has an early discussion of velocity, where he argues that economies of scale will reduce the demand for money relative to income, causing a rising velocity in the long run, that is, he is suggesting that financial sophistication will give velocity an upward trend.[2] Studies in economic development have emphasized the effects of monetization on the demand for money.[3] Friedman–Schwartz consider the effects of financial sophistication as well as of growing security on the demand for money, although they regard these effects as subordinate to the real income effect.

VII. Summary

Wicksell's theory of velocity considers the effects of the rise of bank-produced substitutes for metallic money on the transactions velocity of metallic money. Wicksell had hardly any time series data to work with, still his work provides insights that can be used to explain the secular pattern of velocity. This paper suggests an extension of Wicksell's approach to account for the long-run pat-

---

[1] Barro & Fischer (1976).
[2] Fischer (1911), pp. 79–89.
[3] Gurley & Shaw (1960, pp. 111–12) suggest that financial growth will induce a fall in the income velocity of money, where velocity will approach asymptotically a constant level as the economy matures financially. In the non-econometric literature on the behavior of velocity there are several hypotheses concerning the secular pattern of velocity; it is rising, falling, stable, and various combinations of these trends. See e.g. Selden (1956) and Ezekiel & Adelkunle (1969) for a review of earlier work in this field.

tern of velocity in a number of countries for the period 1870–1970. At one stage of economic development monetization is postulated to have caused a declining trend in the income velocity of notes and deposits. At a later stage financial sophistication coupled with growing security and stability are held to have caused a rising velocity. This Wicksellian hypothesis, which stresses institutional changes, does not exclude the influence of other factors, such as the effects of interest rates and government regulations of money and capital markets, on velocity. These may very well be incorporated as additional factors behind the long-run development of velocity. Empirical tests in the future will reveal the explanatory value of the hypothesis presented here.

References

Anderson, P.: Behavior of monetary velocity. *New England Economic Review*, March/April 1977.

Barro & Fischer: Recent developments in monetary theory. *Journal of Monetary Economics*, April 1976.

Baumol, W.: The transactions demand for cash: An inventory theoretic approach. *Quarterly Journal of Economics*, November 1952.

Ezekiel & Adelkunle: The secular behavior of income velocity: An international cross-section study. *IMF Staff Papers*, July 1969.

Fischer, I.: *The purchasing power of money*. New York, 1911.

Friedman & Schwartz: *A monetary history of the United States 1867–1960*. Princeton, 1963.

Goldsmith, R.: Financial structure and economic growth in advanced countries. In M. Abramovitz (ed.), *Capital formation and economic growth*. Princeton, 1955.

Gurley & Shaw: *Money in a theory of finance*. Washington, 1960.

Johnson, H. G.: Inside money, outside money, income, wealth and welfare in monetary theory. *Journal of Money, Credit and Banking*, February 1969.

Jonung, L.: The behavior of velocity in Sweden 1871–1913. Workshop in Monetary Economics, UCLA 1976.

Klein, B.: Competitive interest payments on bank deposits and the long-run demand for money. *The American Economic Review*, December 1974.

Klein, B.: The demand for quality-adjusted cash balances: Price uncertainty in the U.S. demand for money function. *Journal of Political Economy*, August 1977.

Latané, H. A.: Cash balances and interest rates: A pragmatic approach. *Review of Economics and Statistics*, November 1954.

Latané, H. A.: Income velocity and interest rates: A pragmatic approach. *Review of Economics and Statistics*, November 1960.

Meltzer, A.: The demand for money: The evidence from the time series. *Journal of Political Economy*, June 1963.

Montgomery, A.: *The rise of modern industry in Sweden*. Stockholm, 1939.

Schwartz, A.: Monetary trends in the United States and the United Kingdom, 1878–1970: Selected findings. *The Journal of Economic History*, March 1975.

Selden, R.: Monetary velocity in the United States. In M. Friedman (ed.), *Studies in the quantity theory of money*. Chicago, 1956.

Tobin, J.: The interest-elasticity of transactions demand for cash. *Review of Economics and Statistics*, August 1956.

Tobin, J.: The monetary interpretation of history. *The American Economic Review*, June 1965.

Wicksell, K.: Guld och sedlar. Några ord om omsättningsmedlens väsen och betydelse. (Gold and bank notes. A few

words about the character and importance of the means of payment.)
Svenska Bankmannaföreningen. Styrelsens och revisorernas berättelser för 1901. Stockholm, 1902.

Wicksell, K.: *Lectures on political economy, II.* London, 1935.

Wicksell, K.: *Interest and prices.* London, 1936.

INTRODUCTION TO THE PUBLICATION OF KNUT WICKSELL'S LECTURES ON THE ECONOMIC CONSEQUENCES OF THE FIRST WORLD WAR (1919)

In our preparations for the Arne Ryde Symposium on the Theoretical Contributions of Knut Wicksell, we made a search for interesting works of Wicksell which had not previously been published or translated into English. In spite of the very large amount of printed notes, articles and books by Knut Wicksell—the bibliography by E. J. Knudtzon and T. Hedlund-Nyström *Knut Wicksells tryckta skrifter 1868–1950* (The Publications of Knut Wicksell, 1868–1950)[1,2] contains more than 800 items—the archives at the Lund University Library were found to hide many largely unknown, handwritten manuscripts of Wicksell, mostly fairly complete notes to courses or lectures. The mimeographed publication which we presented at the symposium[2] contains Wicksell's notes to his lectures in Uppsala in 1919 on "The World War: An Economist's View" (*Världskriget ur ekonomisk synpunkt*), and his notes to a series of lectures in Stockholm in 1889, "On Value, Capital and Interest according to Modern Economic Theories". We also included a translated version of the first chapter of the first edition (1901) of Wicksell's "Lectures on Political Economy", which for some particular reason had never been translated into English.

Wicksell's lecture notes on the economic consequences of the First World War are published in this special issue of *The Scandinavian Journal of Economics*, along with a foreword by Bengt Reuterskiöld and Michael D. Bordo, who edited and translated Wicksell's notes. This series of lectures is remarkable in several respects. In this popular exposition, it is impressive to observe the natural ease and pedagogical efficiency with which Wicksell uses his (and Böhm-Bawerk's) theoretical concept of capital as stored-up labor and land services to explain the tremendous outburst of productive power during the war years and the great difficulties of restoring capitalistic production to a pre-war level after 1918. Of course it is also very interesting to follow the thorough and varied argumentation of this old Malthusian thinker on the significance of the changes caused by the war in the size and structure of the population; and to read his quite optimistic considerations on the prospects for the League of Nations.

Lund, November, 1977

Björn Thalberg

---

[1] Lund, 1976.
[2] Available on request from the Institute of Economics, Fack, S-220 05 Lund, Sweden.

THE WORLD WAR: AN ECONOMIST'S VIEW

Knut Wicksell

Translated and edited by Bengt Reuterskiöld and Michael D. Bordo

Foreword

In 1919, the University of Uppsala resumed its summer courses which had been cancelled during the war years. The newspapers, which during the summer carried advertisements for these courses, also contained news about the final terms for peace offered by the Allied Powers to Austria, the discovery of a corpse believed to be that of Rosa Luxemburg, the downfall of Bela Kun, a battle between the British and bolshevik navies in the Gulf of Finland, as well as warnings to the Swedish public to be wary of false banknotes, forged by the bolshevik regime. At the same time the newspapers had to make significant reductions in their editions because a wave of strikes had hit them, begun by a typographers' strike.

"People interested in self-education, teachers and schoolmistresses at secondary and lower schools and folk high-schools, priests and everyone who believes he can benefit from our teaching" were invited to a program of lectures. The list was headed by

A. The Nature of Christianity, from a Historical and Fundamental Point of View.
B. Times of Crisis, from a Historical and Economic Point of View.

Close to five hundred interested persons participated in the two-week program. The crisis series was undoubtedly a good decision. Various well-known scholars, including the Rector of the University himself, lectured on Times of Crisis from Antiquity through the Great Nordic War of Charles XII to the Napoleonic era. And, according to the advertisements, the series was to be rounded off by Professor K. Wicksell's address on "Crisis from an Economic Perspective".

Among the literary remains of Knut Wicksell there is a manuscript entitled "Lectures at the Summer Courses in Uppsala, August, 1919. The Great War from an Economic Point of View". Although no reports of these lectures can be found in the newspapers, which may be explained by their strike-reduced editions, there can be no doubt that this is the manuscript on which the above-mentioned lectures were based.

The text contains Wicksell's own notes for the lectures. It is not a continuous text meant to be read aloud, even less to be published. The contents are such, however, that publication is justified.

The text has by and large been rendered as it stands, no attempt has been made to transform it into normal prose.

Certain difficulties were met with that should be mentioned. The manuscript is of course in longhand and sometimes indistinct, additions had been inserted by the author, and in at least one instance it has not been possible to ascertain what he meant. Apparently Wicksell never made any language revisions.

The sentences progress at a gait which can be termed German professorial and at times without reins. In such instances we have doubted both the possibility and advisability of trying to render the meandering of main and subordinate clauses into a foreign language. In these cases we have attempted some rewriting and in some places verbs have been added to make the text intelligible. However, care has been taken to try to preserve the general tone of the lecture notes.

Readers are thus invited to peer over the shoulder of the seventy year old Wicksell as he sets out on one of his many public lectures, utilizing his own scientific reasearch in the interpretation of current events, reminding himself when to inject a note of sentimentality but leaving little doubt as to when we are to take his idealism seriously.

In these lectures Wicksell conveys his views on important economic, political and social issues of his day. Of special interest to the modern historian of thought is Wicksell's treatment of income generation and the concept of capital in the first lecture, his treatment of the international monetary system in the second, his discussion of the benefits of free trade, international cooperation and the self-sufficiency argument for protection in the third, and finally the population question in the fourth.

In the first lecture Wicksell effectively spells out the problem of reallocating scarce resources from peaceful production and consumption to war purposes. This reallocation, especially if it involves neglect in maintaining both physical and human capital, he pointed out, has serious consequences for the future capital stock of warring states. In the second lecture, he argues the case for a flexible exchange rate for those nations engaged in inflationary war finance, while at the same time he argues that those nations which can maintain stable price levels have no reason to leave the gold standard. Of interest here is Wicksell's suggestion that the Bank of Sweden (the *Riksbank*) should first be allowed to accept interest paying deposits from the public, after which it should raise interest rates in order to reduce the money stock, while simultaneously allowing the exchange rate to float.

In the third lecture, he discusses the gains to all nations from international cooperation through the League of Nations. He also briefly discusses the Ricardian theory of comparative advantage. Then he considers the self-suffiency argument for protection (long adhered to by Sweden) and dismisses it in the light of his hopes for world harmony.

In the fourth lecture he states his long held views of overpopulation—

blaming population pressure for the war and most social conflict. He argues that the population losses of the Great War coupled with the reduction in potential population should provide a sufficient reduction in pressure to allow the League to maintain world peace.

These lectures are of interest to the modern economist because of their relevance to many current world issues, because they tie together many ideas exposed in Wicksell's earlier writings, and finally because they contain an insight into the mind of this great man at the twilight of his career.

Michael D. Bordo
Carleton University, Ottawa, Canada

Bengt Reuterskiöld
University of Lund, Lund, Sweden

THE WORLD WAR: AN ECONOMIST'S VIEW

Knut Wicksell

I

Economic Prerequisites and Consequences of the World War

The study of economic phenomena during the world war contains a gold mine for future economists. The most remarkable item is *the war itself* as an economic accomplishment—a fact unforseen by economists despite Lord Kitchener's (The British Minister of War) prediction of a duration of at least three years.[1]

The Economic Feasibility of the War

The war was essentially a war of positions. However, this is an insufficient explanation. The tremendous increase of expenditures (food, clothes, ammunition etc.) required by the war and the reduction of available productive power (in Austria up to 80 % of those liable to military service, 18–50 years of age, were called up by the middle of 1918) inevitably calls for a corresponding reduction in consumption or an increase in production on the part of the civilian population. The former reduction has undoubtedly taken place. (This is evident in unprecedented privation bordering on starvation and famine, particularly among the countries of the Central Powers.) That the latter increase has occurred is evident in the fullest utilization of the labour of women, children and old men, the extension of the working day, and the abolition of the Sabbath rest.

This in itself is not an adequate explanation. In addition another important factor should be stressed: the *capitalistic nature* of present day production (the word "capitalistic" is not being used here in its *socialist* meaning as denoting ownership of the means of production by the few while the masses remain unpropertied, but rather in the economic sense, as expressing the fact that production to an ever greater extent is directed toward the future). Capital proper (distinguished from natural resources) in all its various shapes (land improvement, cattle, machines and tools, buildings, ships, railways and railway equipment, as well as *stocks* of finished and semi-finished goods) represents on final account, saved or stored up labour or natural resources. When labour is aided in production by capital, then capital is not an increment

---

[1] Wicksell apparently refers to the opinion generally held at the beginning of the war that the war could only last for a few months because of the effects of mass mobilization.

in addition to labour (and natural resources) but is in itself labour and natural resources in another form. Capital must continually be replaced as it is used and worn out (or more than replaced if population grows) and the amount of labour and natural resources needed for this purpose does not satisfy present consumption. On final account each year has, for fulfillment of its own consumption needs, only one vintage or "yearly increment" of labour and natural resources—exactly as in the case of primitive production. But there is a difference in that this increment now to a great extent is composed of labour and natural resources from earlier periods, whereas the greater part of presently available labour and natural resources are used up in preparation for future production.

During the war accumulated capital is exploited at the expense of the future. However, if it is a question of releasing the greatest possible outpouring of economic strength at the present time, which would be decisive for the outcome of the war, then all of the accumulated capital *can* be used more or less for the needs of the moment. One can at the same time spend the treasures of the past and the resources of the present—but only at the expense of the future.

First to be utilized are the accumulated stocks of commodities (in Germany they amounted to, according to Cassel, including livestock, 30 milliards of marks at the old value). Next, fixed capital such as factories and equipment built for other purposes can be adapted for production of the requirements of war. Finally we observe the withholding of the normal replacement of capital—buildings not repaired or constructed, rails and ties as far as possible not being replaced and the exhaustion of agricultural land.

The Consequences of these Developments for the Immediate Future
It is possible in the above way for an enormous economic expansion to take place during a few years in exactly those countries which have advanced the farthest in material culture and capitalistic production. But this can only be achieved at the expense of the future and only to the extent that this outpouring has been great and has had the potential to be great in the past. For, after peace is finally restored and production and consumption return once more to their normal paths, then the prerequisites of capitalistic production will be missing since all stocks will have been depleted, all machines and parts, buildings and so forth will have been altered for the use of war and partly worn out to the outmost degree. (Aside—elaborate on the importance of inventories for production.) Now all this must be replaced, inventories to be replenished, machines and buildings to be repaired, not to speak of the destruction in the ares of combat which fortunately are not very vast, before normal production can take place. Normal production can only be purchased for the next few years of peace by a continuation of greatly reduced consumption. One could possibly believe that a country which has been capable of great

exertion during the war would also have a corresponding capacity for rapid recovery after the war, but the opposite should be the case. (Russia, less capitalistic, withdrew from the war sooner and perhaps shall recover before the others.) To live in a primitive way, from hand to mouth, is impossible in the densely populated highly capitalistic countries.

This is the real danger that threatens the world in the near future (it would be a good thing if this danger could be somewhat alleviated by peaceful cooperation among nations). The colossal debts of war that burden all the warring states, represent properly speaking, only a symptom of reality, certainly not the reality itself. As a matter of fact they only represent a claim on the treasury (e.g., on the taxpayers by certain other individuals (possibly in another country)). If these claims were evenly distributed, they would *as such* have no influence at all. But the reality behind the transfer of real capital from productive activity to a use where it acts in the service of destruction and is itself destroyed—this reality no compensation can undo.

To this must be added the unprecedented destruction of human material itself. Not only the cripples but all the participants of the war return marked for life by a ruined nervous system or bad health. In the civilian population you observe malnutrition, especially fatal in childhood, tuberculosis etc. Finally you observe the problem of the widespread dispersion of venereal diseases.

The direct and indirect *losses of human life* during the war (fallen on the battlefield, increased mortality in the civilian population and decreased birthrate during the war) are given primary importance by many observers. (According to Döhring, *Selskab för social forskning*, Bulletin II, the postwar population in Germany and Austria–Hungary together is about 10.82 millions less than it would have been, had there been no war.) But this matter has from a pure economic perspective, as shall be demonstrated later on in these lectures, two sides.

From a social point of view there is to be noted first the great number of widows and orphans as the calling up to war duty has been extended so high up in the age groups, and second among youth, the serious disproportion between young men and women. For instance in Austria–Hungary, before the war there were 1 000 men between 20 and 30 years of age corresponding to 1 052 women of the same age. As 20 % of these young men have been lost in the war, the proportion should now be: men 1 000, women 1 315. From a human standpoint, this can be seen in the tears of the unfortunate mothers and other surviving relatives. This presents an extremely sombre picture, which would be cause for despair were it not for the hope of it changing to a brighter future.

The neutral countries have in every respect had a more lucky escape. But we will certainly not be spared of all influence from the difficult conditions of production abroad. (International trade is mainly an exchange of different products not a competition with products of the same kind.) As far as our own country is concerned, we have used up a great amount of real capital—although with one great difference—that as a nation we have been compensated for this and thus accordingly we ought to be able to procure real capital in exchange for our monetary claims. The unfortunate thing is: a) that these claims are possessed by a relative minority of the population of the country; and b) that their real value is in doubt. In this connection, there are two further questions which complicate the problems of the world war and the peace: (1) the colossal transfer of property, between individuals, and (2) the neglected state into which the world's monetary system has fallen during the war and as a consequence of the war. The first of these questions can be mentioned here only in passing, but the second is to be dealt with at length in the next lecture.

II

The Monetary System, Increases in the Price Level and the Exchange Rate during and after the War

Dear Times during a War are not an Absolute Necessity

War and dear times are two afflictions that usually come together. On first view, this is self evident. The need for practically all goods is increased during the war whereas the supply decreases, unless foreign credits (or existing stocks) can meet the shortage. Housing is well nigh the only consumption good to which this does *not* apply (in fact rents actually fell during the war, for instance in Germany). However, a strong need is not sufficient for an increase in the price of a commodity. In addition there must be *effective purchasing power*. Were it possible to decrease the purchasing power of the civilian population to the same extent as the government's has been increased, then a powerful drag would have been put on price increases. This can be done, at least in theory, with the aid of taxes and loans (within the country). (To be expanded Wagner's system of war taxes, loans for subscription at extremely high interest rates.) To be sure, even so general a price increase could not be avoided if the quantity of goods had been reduced in relation to the existing quantity of money (the quantity theory of money, which to a great extent has been confirmed during the war) but in that case the inflation would have been trifling—some tens of percent. This holds for the general price level, as well as certain particularly essential goods: provisions (if not rationed), fuel etc. would probably rise *more* in price, while other commodities, not just rents, would fall in price.

The Emission of Paper Money

Now, warring states have in all times made use of another means to procure the necessary purchasing power: increases in the quantity of money. [Aside:

the collecting of treasures in ancient times. The war treasure of Charles XI of 1.2 million daler silvercoins was spent (together with the liquid assets in the treasurer's office) by Charles XII. During the 18th and 19th centuries the same thing happened on a much larger scale through the emission *en masse* of bank notes and government paper money. (Sweden in the beginning of the 18th and 19th centuries, the French "assignats", the Danish "kurant" notes during the Napoleonic war, confederate currency during the North-American civil war. During the civil war in the republic of Columbia in the eighteen nineties the paper peseta fell in only a few years from one dollar to one cent.] In this way governmental borrowing is to a large extent facilitated because holders of goods, and businessmen, who earn excessive profits as a result of the rise in prices, place these gains at the government's disposal by subscribing for governmental loans. But in reality it is the great public that in the first instance has to subscribe for these loans through their privation—they starve for the money and, in addition, later on in the future they pay the interest and amortization on these loans with their taxes, which they by compulsion have saved up for, but from which other people have benefitted. (For instance take the wholesale dealer in hides with stocks worth 100 000 crowns—what would have happened if the government *from the beginning* had borrowed from the public to pay for the leather.)

Take the case of a small region at war, with a gold 'agio' [premium] and a deterioration of the exchange rate. Now, if the war is restricted to a smaller region the consequence of the above mentioned will be that the value of the paper currencies of the warring states will fall not only in relation to commodities but also in relation to the precious metals (gold and silver, nowadays mainly gold) on which the currency system of other states still rest. Gold will flow out of the country or will have to be kept back by artificial means; paper money will have to be declared irredeemable, if this has not been done from the beginning, and will reach a lower value in relation to gold and the essentially unaltered currencies of other countries. The decrease of paper money in relation to gold is called a 'disagio' (discount) and it manifests itself as a deterioration of the exchange rate with foreign countries. (To be worked out later on.) The price level in other countries and hence the *world price level* will thus remain almost unaltered. But in the warring countries, which by now have a depreciated paper currency, prices will have risen, to be sure, but only in terms of paper money. They will remain practically unaltered in terms of gold—to the extent that such a relation is still applicable (after the war the country has to raise its notes to the old parity).

The World War, General Inflation, No or Uncertain Gold Agio
However, if the war comprises a great, or the greater part of the world, as has been the case, the result will be different. If then there is a great emission of notes in all or most countries (including the neutral) and there is an ensuing

rise in prices (inflation) gold will have no reason to travel to one place more than to another, even if gold exports are unrestricted. Bank notes can still be kept redeemable (at least if it is insured so that there exists a supply of low denomination notes as has been the case in our country) no gold 'agio' will occur, there will be no alteration of exchange rates from par, and everything can seemingly go on as under the full gold exchange standard, which in actual fact it has not been necessary to abandon. Yet even under these conditions there still can occur a tremendous rise in prices and deterioration of the purchasing power of money. The value of gold has fallen together with the value of bank notes.

Certainly the actual development of the currency systems of the world shows in its details a very different picture. The value of money has in some countries fallen considerably more than in others and as a result exchange rates have fallen far below par and have fluctuated greatly (for instance with Germany). As far as gold is concerned there has hardly existed a free gold market since the beginning of the war to the present (we ourselves have been redeeming notes since January 1916 but gold exports on private account is still barred). Hence, it is in reality impossible to tell the value of gold, or rather, what its value would be were the free exchange of gold to be resumed. But there is hardly any doubt that the value of gold would turn out to be scarcely worth more than banknotes in countries now having the most favourable exchange rates (Austria, The Netherlands, Sweden) and perhaps not even that. (Digression on the exchange rate.)

Naturally under these conditions gold production is scarcely profitable. Golddiggers or goldmining companies can only produce a given quantity of gold per day or per year, which now corresponds to perhaps one half or one third its initial value in terms of commodities. Were the high price level to continue, gold mining must be reduced to only the most profitable mines. Were it now as before the war, when gold was used in commerce (instead of notes) by the great trading countries: England, France, Germany etc., then this relative scarcity of gold would soon exert downward pressure on the emission of bank notes and lead to a fall in prices. But now even these countries have turned to the use of nothing but paper (with the exception of silver subsidiary coinage) in commerce, and gold only in the banks. In this case very little gold is needed. Only if gold production dwindles to the extent that industrial demand for it cannot be met, and industrial users have to turn to the bank supply would the banks then sooner or later have to reduce their emission of notes, but this may take a long time. Consequently there is no compelling reason for a continuing fall in prices after the war, nor do sizeable outstanding government debts call for an increase in the value of money (to be worked out) although the matter could be dealt with by an appropriate and just writing down of all debts incurred at a lower value of money. (As opposed to the dissolution of all earlier property relations.)

Some General Reflections particularly with regard to Swedish Conditions

Money is a medium of exchange, a measure of the exchange value of commodities. The ideal thing would evidently be to make this measure, like all other measures, as invariant as possible. ("The King's better measure", Jevons). The exchange values of the precious metals *in the last resort* is dependent upon (or at least consistent with) the amount of labour (or "labour and capital") necessary to produce a certain quantity of gold, for example one gram. But this quantity of labour is variable, since it can: (1) be diminished by the discovery of new goldfields or improved techniques in goldmining or be augmented by the exhaustion of the gold fields. In addition, (2) the amount of labour can vary at any given point of time as the various mines have different productivity. Thus the so called marginal cost of gold production is decisive in determining the exchange value of gold but this very margin is alterable according to the greater or lesser need for gold by the banks and industry. Finally, (3) the conditions of gold production must in *the long-run* delimit the value of money and the general level of prices in a monetary system based on gold, but during shorter periods of a few years or even decades this factor can be neutralized by the influence from currency and credit policy, even if full convertibility of bank notes and other bank assets into gold is maintained. In this connection it is also true that a single country cannot possibly protect itself against an inflation or a rise in prices caused by a strong issue of notes in many other countries as long as it has to freely mint gold or give up its notes against gold in a fixed relation.

These imperfections in the gold standard will undoubtedly give rise to a more rational monetary system in the future, when central banks simply will have to limit their issue of bank-notes to such an extent that the value of money and hence the average level of commodity prices will be held constant. It is of interest to note that we ourselves have had approximately such a system for more than three years now, although we are still to some extent tied by the currency union with Norway and Denmark.

Our Present Monetary System

In February, 1916 the free minting of gold was abolished and so was the central bank's obligation to accept gold in exchange for 2 480 crowns in terms of notes (less 1/4 %). The same measure was taken in Norway and Denmark but without any further collaboration in currency policy. Thus gold could still be minted in Norway and Denmark (and with the consent of their governments be sent here in the shape of gold coins. But even this was prevented by agreement, although not until the fall of 1917). In reality our central bank is sovereign with regard to the value of money and the general price level in Sweden. The means for achieving this is by controlling the level of the rate of interest of money (the discount rate) but this means would be still more potent if the central bank were allowed to accept interest paying deposits. By increasing the interest rates for loans and deposits the central bank can decrease the stock of bank notes in circulation at its own discretion and force down the average price level to any level no matter how low, and [it can do this] totally independent of how high prices are abroad. (Naturally our exchange rates with foreign countries will then fall correspondingly.)

As has been pointed out, this [analysis] applies to the *average* price level not for individual commodity prices. It would still be possible to influence these, at least to a certain degree, if the government had levied adequate export duties on our export commodities during the war, and used the funds thus collected to subsidize the sales of imported goods below their cost-price (to be worked out).

However, none of these measures were resorted to, with the results we have before us; and unfortunately it is impossible to discern any definite course or avenues of direction for our monetary system. Apparently our leaders are dominated by the view that money takes care of itself if it is only left on its own—but unfortunately this is not the case.

III

The League of Nations as a Factor in the World Economy

We now turn from this more or less gloomy view of the immediate future to the fortunately much brighter picture which is held out for the subsequent period. The most promising thing in this connection is undeniably the League of Nations—if only its promise could be fulfilled. This ought not to be impossible. It should be possible to avoid war among nations, as well as civil war and insurrection, more easily in the former case than the latter because civil war and insurrection are caused by profound social conflicts. In the case of international conflict, with one exception, there are no conflicting interests that cannot be settled in a peaceful way. This sole exception is the population problem (next lecture). If this problem could be solved, the various nations of the world would live as peacefully together as the different provinces in one country or as do people from all parts of the world now living in the United States.

The Disappearance of the Military Budget

What influence would this have on the economic conditions of the world? The first, and in itself most important consequence, would be the removal for each country of the intolerable economic burden caused by the costs of armament before the war. If this could be achieved fairly rapidly, then this fact alone would go a long way towards healing the wounds caused by the war. Whereas in earlier times, after a war, nations usually started rearming with doubled energy in an attempt to keep their gains or to recoup their losses.

The League of Nations (in its present imperfect state) is a factor for mutual aid during the initial years of peace.

Second, comes the probable development of international economic relations. It has already been mentioned that the difficult transition period would demand a certain amount of international co-operation in order to surmount the greatest difficulties in procuring the necessities of life. Even after this transition period one ought to count upon a continuing and accentuated development of international agreements with an economic purpose, following developments started before the war: The Postal Union, similar arrangements for telegraphy. Also the use of the railway network is now to a large extent on an international scale.

The League of Nations and Free Trade

Still, the most important question is: will international trade be favourably influenced by a state of secure peace?

One could be doubtful about the prospects for peace if the Allies continue to maintain the boycott of the Central Powers that began during the war (The Paris Conference of 1916). But it must be remembered that an important consideration for the Allies is to protect themselves against new attacks from the Germans. If such aggressive tendencies still abide within the German people and their potential allies, then there exists no other means than trying to keep down economically the potential enemy. Even we should prepare ourselves for certain retaliations. If however, Germany should give unmistakeable proof of an honest intention towards peace and be admitted to the League of Nations then these causes for continued protectionism should disappear. However, that does not mean that free trade will be attained, since it is likely that each country, particularly the economically feeble, would find reason to protect itself with tariff walls and the like acting in its *own* interest (and not necessarily to damage its opponent).

Protectionism and Militarism

In this connection one should consider to what extent protectionism is connected with considerations of national defense. Why else should there be this total contrast between complete free trade and liberty to pursue a trade *within* each country and the thousands of obstacles against trade in international intercourse.

International Trade: Exchange not Competition

What is international trade? Evidently a division of labour on a grand scale. Here there is a contrast between the views from the private economic and national economic prospectives. The individual exporter considers himself first and last as a competitor on the foreign market; the domestic producer fears competition from abroad in "his" market. But by and large international trade is of course not competition between similar products but exchange of heterogeneous products, where each country has its own speciality.

(An arithmetic example of comparative costs.) Ricardo's cobbler and hatter. The division of labour is advantageous to both even if one is more skillful in both branches, if only his superiority is more pronounced in one of them. This is its general conception (even though strongly simplified). But if they live in animosity or expect it, it is advisable for both to make their own shoes and hats.

The Argument for Economic Isolation for Protective Tariffs

This in reality is one of the strongest arguments for protection. A country should not to an excessive degree specialize in its production, because if it becomes isolated by war it will run into distress. But even in this respect, the world war has made it evident that reorganization of production to self-sufficiency is much easier then used to be believed—of course with the exception of those commodities a country *cannot* produce at all. However if the danger of isolation through war disappears this argument loses its force. It is a bit late *now* to argue for self-sufficiency, but during the war a reorganization of our production towards self-sufficiency *could* have been made.

But there are two more arguments for tariffs: one social (agricultural vs industrial tariffs); and another, that in most cases is more instinctively felt than clearly conceived. The *internal* freedom and liberty to pursue a trade trade has resulted in a considerable migration of the population in each country. Some areas have become very densely populated while other areas are more sparsely populated or even depopulated. From a national point of view this involves no real disadvantage: you are a *Swede* whether you live in Stockholm, Scania or Laplandia. But free international trade has doubtless produced the same tendency, for example: suppose that lumber and paper prices continue to be very high while the prices of grain and other provisions return to their pre-war level. (Not entirely improbable, as the world supply of lumber incessantly diminishes while grain harvests do not diminish.) The result would then have to be that with the exception of some particularly favoured agricultural districts, the most advantageous thing from an agricultural point of view would be to let all arable land, meadows and pasture grow into forest. (Janne and his crofter.)

But of course forestry could, even in combination with industries based on it only nourish part of the present population in the country—the remainder would have to emigrate. From the point of view of the world economy this would be best, and also from the viewpoint of the Swedish national economy. (e.g. Two brothers who jointly own a homestead suitable for forestry—the one keeps the homestead and runs a timber business, the other takes his share in cash, which is greater than he would receive were he to continue farming, and emigrates.) But form a *national* point of view, from the point of view of the country's military defense this would be questionable and one would probably try to prevent it with the aid of agricultural tariffs. But if the need for military defence disappears—and with us perhaps it is more the anxious feeling of insecurity—then even this argument ceases *essentially* to be valid.

By and large, the League of Nations should lead to the weakened importance of national boundaries and ultimately to their final abolition. Even in this respect reservation certainly has to be made for the influence of the population question, to which we will return in the next lecture. (Digression on nationalism: nationalism really is equal to the ability to read coupled with ignorance of all languages other than ones own.) When we speak of human beings in other planets we think of them as one people. In reality the attempts in this direction are more far reaching than surmised—if only the devil of war could be definitely expunged from the earth.

IV

The War and the Population Problem

I mentioned in my last lecture that all sorts of strife between nations, with the exception of one, are of such a nature that it would be possible to settle them in a peaceful way by agreement or at worst by arbitration. The sole exception is strife over territory. If a people becomes too numerous for its territory and sees no other way out for its survival than to extend its dominion at the cost of its neighbour, then it is hard to see how such strife could be solved by agreement. An arbitrator should in this case probably conclude that each nation should stay within its own boundaries, but that would be no solution and the trouble would remain.

Unfortunately, this is the very strife that in all periods has constituted the foremost if not the only reason for war. There is no doubt about this as far as earlier times are concerned (the ravages of the Vikings etc.). The wars of that time were pure wars of extermination, but, unless they ended too unhappily, they brought relief even to the vanquished—hence they were popular. In medieval times and later on one has generally tried to disguise or embellish the naked purpose of conquest, thus at times wars have been labelled crusades, at times religious wars, at times wars of independence and so on, and of course to some extent they have been just that, but on closer inspection it will turn out that even in these cases it has ultimately been the lack of space to feed the population that has given rise to seething discontent, which is the necessary background and sounding-board for military enterprises. (The American civil war: the abolition of negro slavery an effect but not the cause.) The governing classes in a country are almost always more or less prone to war if only there is chance of victory because their own raison d'être really rests on the military structure of the society (the capitalists as well—hence Wagner's war taxes). The broad masses are mostly of a more peaceful mind, but their will for peace gets weakened when the struggle for existence becomes a more hardfought one, and in the end makes them inclined for a change of whatever kind.

War and Increase in Population a Circulus Vitiosus
In addition there is the fact that this connection between war and increases in population is a double one. Throughout history increases in population and wars condition each other in an eternal *circulus vitiosus*. For if on the one hand overcrowding creates the necessity and longing for a war, a numerous population on the other hand is a prerequisite for victory. Therefore steps to check the increase in population in a peaceful way by decreasing birth-rates will always encounter resistance among the ruling and military classes; and at the end of a war, be it won or lost, nothing is generally considered more important than to encourage a strong increase in population in order to "fill the cadres" again.

The Reduction of Population in Germany during the War
Before the war Germany was severely threatened by overpopulation, the feverish industrial development certainly could not have continued for long at the same rate—in 20 years a doubling in the production of coal, a fourfold increase in production of lignite, a threefold increase in pig-iron—this was admitted by the Germans themselves and was openly given as one of the main reasons for the war—(the same goes for Austria). According to Fried the actual and potential decrease in population amounts to no less than 8 million. But that is not the end of it, the millions of men, mostly unmarried or newly married, that lie on the battlefield or are disabled to such an extent that they are incapable of providing for themselves would under normal circumstances have married before long and raised children in small or great numbers—these will now fail to appear. For Germany this is no doubt a bright feature in the general disaster: the population problem that on the one hand already existed and on the other was bound to occur in Germany has now to a considerable extent been eased for the near future, although the ensuing maldistribution of population for the time being is a drawback. But far from appreciating this the ruling circles are only evolving plans for replacing this "loss" as soon as possible by increased birth-rates.

Checking the Population Increase as an Indispensable Condition for World Peace
There can be no doubt that if a population increase were to occur in all the countries of the world on the same scale as during the past century, all hopes

for a world peace would be in vain. The stomach is a stern ruler, against its demands all treaties are anulled. (At the Russian–Finnish frontier it has come to the point where slain enemies are cooked and eaten—just like in the oldest times of humanity—and warfare.)

Fortunately, the prospects for this condition to be fulfilled by degrees are not poor. The great peace organization, the League of Nations, is in itself to a certain degree a guarantee for this, at least to the extent that the menace of war can no longer be given as a reason by those who advocate a perpetual increase in population in the various countries. If population increase and war form a circulus vitiosus, then population control and peace ought to form a circulus favorabilis.

An even more hopeful fact that made its appearance in the decades preceding the world war in well-nigh all civilized countries is the spontaneous movement for a decrease in birth-rates, and it will certainly not cease to act after the war. The movement was prominent not least in Germany. Although the growth of the German population had not yet noticeably started to decline, the birth-rate had ceased increasing and instead had declined in absolute numbers, a fact that naturally would have led to a decrease in the younger age classes. (From 1916 the number of school children in the lower forms would not have increased any further even if there had been no war.) However paradoxically as it may sound, it is quite probable (Öhrvall) that this circumstance gave the military party cause for striking as soon as possible. In about 25 years (from 1914) the population of Germany would have become stationary (Bortkievich). As a result of the war this will probably happen *now*, and hence one should be able to depend upon the same love for peace within the German nation as within the French—even without a League of Nations and à fortiori with it.

Population Control and the Social Question
With the cessation of the growth of population, prerequisites are created for a successful settlement of the social question, which quite likely will come to the forefront when it no longer is disturbed by political strife among the nations. The social question is briefly: (*a*) a wages-question (the 8-hour working day is also mainly a wages-question); and (*b*) a question of the distribution of property. When the supply of workers becomes more limited then (*a*) labour will be more valuable and wages will rise, while capitalists and landowners will have to be content with less. (The relative amount of capital will increase and the rate of return on capital will fall; with soil-improvement the tilled area will increase and rent will fall.) But (*b*) one has to pursue a more just distribution of property (the German property tax and Ebert's promise to confiscate war profits) for instance, by creating funds for the welfare of the working class, sickness- old age-, unemployment insurance. Obviously these measures are more easily carried out and more promising the less numerous is the unproprieted class.

Socialization will not solve the problem. It is an excellent measure and should also, according to my view, without doubt be adopted whenever an industry shows a tendency towards high concentration, monopoly or trust-formation, but hardly before that. Socialization is then foremost a technical question. But a measure that is prompted by equity and fairness should evidently not be postponed while waiting for a certain technical development that perchance will be late in coming or never come to certain branches of economic activity (agriculture).

The State of Affairs in Sweden

Concluding Remarks

The number of newborn in Sweden is scarcely sufficient to maintain the present numbers in the age groups of 20–30 years. Under such conditions the population will still increase for some time, but thereafter decrease. It is however unlikely that its number will fall to zero. There is a special reason to wish a decrease in population in Sweden. At present, certain of our natural resources are undoubtedly overtaxed. But after a moderate decrease in population (for instance to 3 million) they should suffice to a well-nigh unlimited degree, whereas in other countries the abatement of the coalseams will necessitate a far more considerable reduction of the stock of population.

But small or large, the main thing is that our population, and the world's, will have the opportunity for a happy and rich life befitting human beings, that is among other things, a *peaceful* life.

INTRODUCTION TO KNUT WICKSELL'S "THE THEORY OF POPULATION, ITS COMPOSITION AND CHANGES"

Wicksell's "The Theory of Population, its Composition and Changes" is published here for the first time in English. It was originally the first chapter in the first Swedish edition of his *Lectures on Political Economy, Volume I* (1901). Wicksell was of the express opinion that a standard textbook on political economy should begin with a chapter on population.[1] Moreover, Wicksell's interest in this field was indeed very strong; he considered the problem of population to be "the most important and at the same time the most neglected of all social problems".

However, Wicksell's population chapter did not appear in the later editions of his *Lectures*. In 1910, the chapter—in slightly rewritten form—was published separately as a pamphlet in the Swedish student association Verdandi's pamphlet series. As indicated in Wicksell's own preface below, he prepared this edition in Ystad prison, while serving a two-month sentence for blasphemy. When the second edition of *Lectures on Political Economy* appeared in 1911, "The Theory of Population, its Composition and Changes" was listed in the table of contents as the first chapter of the book, but the chapter itself was omitted and the reader was referred to the 1910 pamphlet. The population chapter was also omitted from the subsequent editions of Wicksell's *Lectures*, including the English edition of 1934 by L. Robbins (which was based on the third Swedish edition). This translation of the 1910 pamphlet version of Wicksell's population chapter is by Professor Göran Ohlin, Uppsala.[2] Surely, the reader will find that the chapter is not only of historical interest, but that Wicksell's thoughts on the population problem are indeed relevant and of interest also today.

Björn Thalberg
Lund, June 1978

---

[1] See the Introduction in his *Lectures on Political Economy*. He writes here "... it will be found that the theory of population, which can never be omitted from a complete treatise on political economy, can never find a suitable place in the system unless it forms an introduction to the whole" (p. 6).

[2] Knut Wicksell's population chapter was republished in Swedish with a few alterations by his son, Sven Wicksell, in 1926. Here, however, we have chosen to translate Knut Wicksell's own last version of it. Reference should also be made to Monica S. Fong's article in *History of Political Economy* (1976), pp. 311–323, "Knut Wicksell's 'The Two Population Questions'." In her article, Fong comments on Wicksell's writings on population and social problems, and presents a translation of the eighth (and last) section of Wicksell's population chapter.

THE THEORY OF POPULATION, ITS COMPOSITION AND CHANGES

Knut Wicksell

Translated by Göran Ohlin

Preface

This essay originally constituted the first chapter of my published lectures on political economy. As I am presently about to prepare a new edition of Volume I of these lectures, I have with great pleasure accepted an old request from the committee for the pamphlet series of the Verdandi association to publish the first chapter, duly revised, as a pamphlet. The revision concerns mainly the statistical material in the first part of the essay, which has been revised throughout and thus brought up to date as far as possible in conjunction with available statistical publications. Unfortunately, I am not an expert in this field, but since most of the data are taken from official publications, I dare hope that they are largely correct. The latter half of the essay, which contains the real scientific (Malthusian) theory of population, has not been altered, with the exception that several objections to the Malthusian theory have been briefly answered.

As a complement to my exposition below, I permit myself to refer to my verdict regarding Sweden's emigration problem, which I have written about at the request of the Commission on Emigration, and which might soon be available in the Commission's printed series.

The work on this pamphlet has provided pleasant diversion during my enforced idleness. My hope is that it may widely increase knowledge on the population problem, the most important and at the same time the most neglected of all social problems.

Knut Wicksell
Ystad Jail, October 1909

I
The Age Distribution

Looking at the different age groups in an actual population, e.g. our own, one finds that they always decline in size so that each yearly, or at least quinquennial group is smaller than the immediately preceding one. This state of affairs, which is everywhere observed, is not strictly inevitable, at least not in a stationary population. One could imagine a population living under extremely favourable economic and hygienic conditions in which all individuals attained the physiologically possible age, e.g. 80–100 years. If this population were also stationary, so that year after year the same number of children, say 100,000, were born—which is easily seen to imply that on the average 100,000 old people must die each year—the living population at any point in time would have the structure illustrated in Fig. 1.

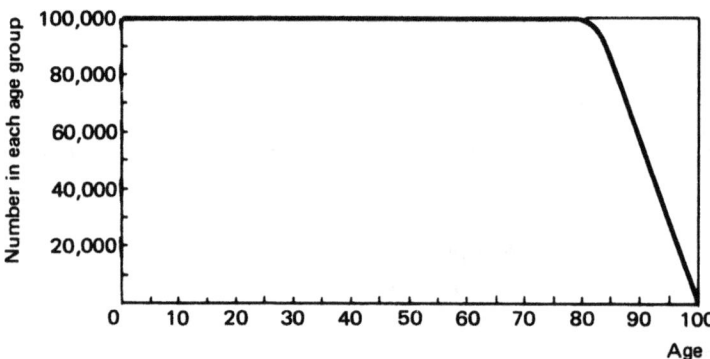

Fig. 1. A stationary population with mortality in higher age groups only

All age groups except the oldest, between 80 and 100, would be equal in size; the size of the total population is easily found to be about 9 million, slightly more or slightly less depending on whether the curve on the right is primarily convex or concave. The annual birth rate would be about 11 per thousand, and the death rate would be the same. The population would be like a river fed from one single source, in which not a drop is lost until the river reaches its estuary. The old age groups would be numerous, and the children would be relatively few although numerous enough to maintain the population. Those over 50 would be $\frac{4}{9}$, those under 15 only $\frac{1}{6}$, and the population between 15 and 50 would be $\frac{7}{18}$ or about 40 per cent of the total.

In reality, as we have already mentioned and as Fig. 3 immediately shows, the picture is quite different, in that the various age groups all decline in size, from the youngest to the oldest. There are several reasons for this. The most important is that death of course takes its toll in all age groups and therefore incessantly reduces them. However, if this were the only reason, the age distribution would be quite different from what it actually is. Thus, in a population with 100,000 births a year and with the mortality in various age groups that was characteristic of Sweden in the decade 1890–1900, the age distribution of the population would look like the curve in Fig. 2. This population would be stationary, for if the number of births remains the same year after year, and also the mortality in the various age groups, then each age group must take

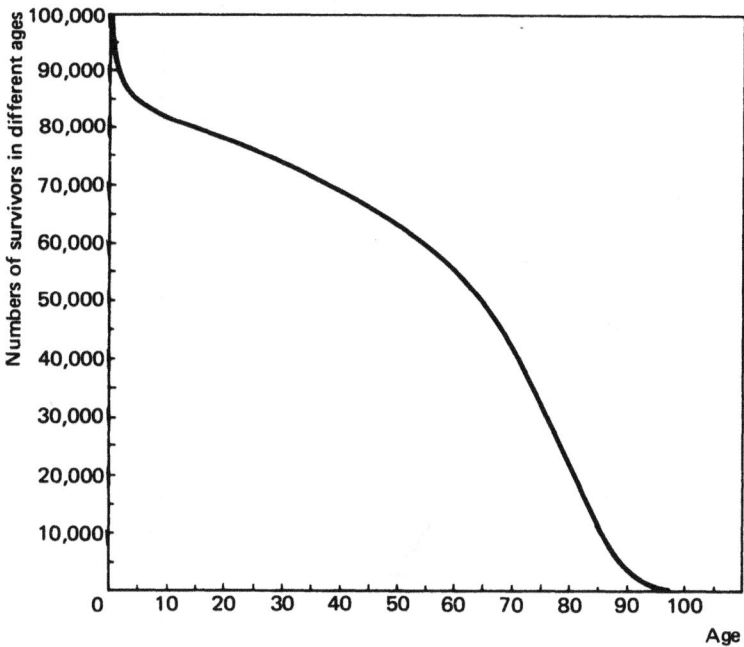

Fig. 2. A stationary population with successive mortality.

on a constant size, corresponding to the annual number of births reduced by all the deaths in the preceding age groups. The number of deaths in all age groups must add up to the number of births, or 100,000. The total population would, on the above assumption about mortality, be about 5¼ million; those under 15 would number about 1¼ million or 24 per cent, those of 15–50 about 2½ million or 48 per cent, those over 50 about 1½ million or 28 per cent. The birth rate as well as the death rate would be 19 per thousand.

If we compare this composition with the actual age distribution as estimated for 1906 on the basis of the census of 1900 (Fig. 3), the discrepancy is striking. The actual number of births is currently about 135,000—as with insignificant variations it has been for more than three decades—but the total population in 1906 was only 5,337,000, or insignificantly more than our hypothetical population above. Of this, the ages 0–15 accounted for 1.7 million or about 32 per cent, those of 15–50 were 2.53 million or about 47½ per cent and only 1.1 million or 20½ per cent were over 50. Whilst the middle group is of approximately the same size in both cases, the young are more numerous and the aged are fewer in the real than in the hypothetical stationary population. One consequence is that the death rate in Sweden in 1890–1900 was only 16½ per thousand, as compared with 19 per thousand in our hypothetical population, and this in spite of our assumption that the mortality in each age bracket would be the

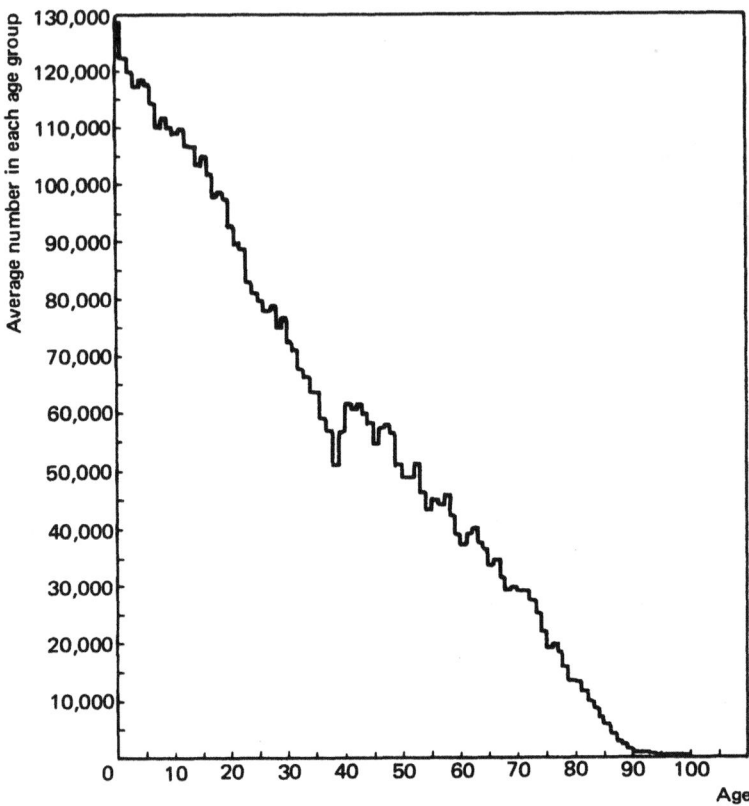

Fig. 3. The actual population in Sweden, 1906.

same. The reason is precisely that the high age groups with higher mortality levels are less common in reality than in the stationary population, while the reverse is true of the younger age groups whose mortality, except in the first year of life, is very low.

The reasons for this discrepancy between the age distributions of the actual population and the stationary population with precisely the same age-specific mortality are of three different kinds: the growth of the population, the secular decline in mortality, and finally emigration.

Like most other countries, Sweden has almost uninterruptedly increased its population in the last century, or, for that matter, since our statistical records began. This must in general imply that the number of births increases from year to year, or at least from decade to decade—only the figures of the last three decades constitute a remarkable exception in this regard. Thus the higher age groups derive from earlier and therefore less numerous cohorts of births than the younger age groups, and will for this reason, too, be smaller. One may illustrate the situation graphically by drawing the survival curve, which is about the same as the curve for the stationary population we have discussed earlier, for the births in each year over a century, say 1806–1906. The composition of the actual population, as determined by the factors we have so far discussed, would be represented by a locus made up of only one point on each of these 101 curves. Fig. 4 is intended to show this, although only every tenth survival curve has been included and for simplicity we have indicated the number of births only in rounded numbers for the extreme years of 1806 and 1906, simply assuming for the intermediate years that births throughout the century increased at a constant geometric rate of about 0.7 per cent per year. The agreement between the curve thus constructed and that of the actual age distribution in Fig. 3 is more apparent than real. In particular, the near constancy of the births in the last decades ought to make the age distribution "swell out" much more in the early years, as it does for the stationary population in Fig. 2.

But now we must add the fact that mortality in the past was considerably higher than now in all age groups; consequently the old, who in part have been exposed to this higher mortality, will have been more depleted than they would have been if mortality had during the whole century been at the level of 1890–1900.

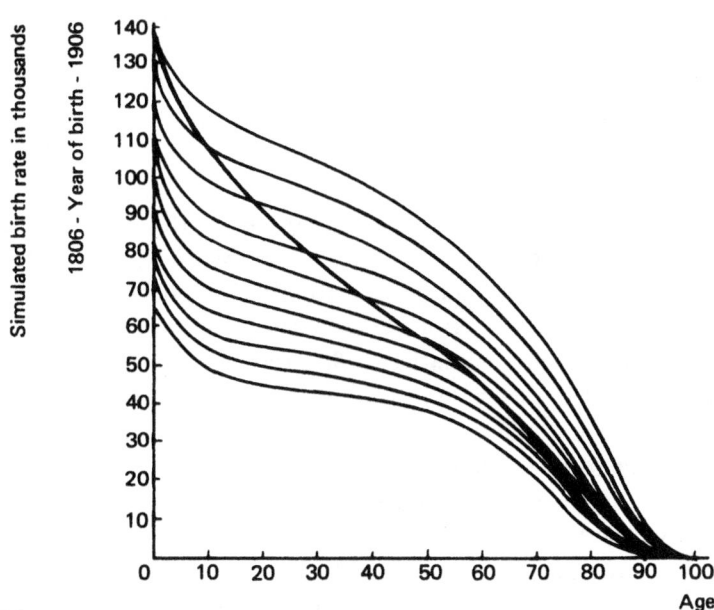

Fig. 4. The effects of a successively increasing birth rate.

Finally, we have to consider emigration. If it were evenly distributed among all age groups, its effect on the age distribution would only be that of a stronger mortality. The curve would decline more steeply but without any change in its general shape. However, as is well known, emigration occurs primarily in the group of 15–35, and most of all in that of 15–25. Large emigration therefore cuts deeply into these age groups which will be decimated in comparison with the younger ones. After emigration has continued for some time, the older age groups too will have been decimated and the right-hand part of the curve will therefore retain its shape, but all groups over 15 and particularly those of young men will be underrepresented in comparison with the childhood groups—although the births will also be affected by the smaller number of women in fertile age.[1]

II
Composition by Sex and Marital Status

For 1000 girls born in Sweden in the years 1897–1906 there were on the average 1057 boys; this ratio is roughly the same in all countries and all periods covered by statistical records. So far no satisfactory explanation has been given of this strange circumstance, but it seems possible that it should be related to the excess mortality of males, either directly through a causal linkage not yet observed,[2] or indirectly as the result of a genetic characteristic which the species has acquired by natural selection. This excess mortality of males is presently found in Sweden through the fourth year of life and then again from the eighteenth year on. It gradually reduces the male excess and in the higher age groups causes an excess of women. However, this process of natural levelling is much slower than it is generally thought to be. It is true that equal numbers obtain in the neighbourhood of 20, but this is entirely due to the fact that far more men than women emigrate, even in the age 15–20. Were it not for this circumstance, the sexes would not become equal in number in Sweden until after 50, and in the countryside a decade later. Thus if emigration ceases, or if it turns into a predominantly female migration as has recently been the case in Sweden certain years, and if the mortality of urban males could be reduced to the level of rural males, there would be a not insignificant excess of males in all ages below 60. As the age of marriage is generally a few years higher for men than for women, this would, among other things, affect the frequency of marriage among women and thereby also the female labour force.

Of even greater importance in this respect are those circumstances, primarily economic, which enable men to marry reasonably young. In this respect, con-

---
[1] The conspicuous drop in the age group 35–40 (Fig. 3) is due to the abnormally low birth rate in the distressed years of 1867–68 and following. Such demographic waves—in this case a trough or a drought, in others a crest or a flood—are not uncommon and may, if sufficiently pronounced, be the cause of social transformations of which it is important to be aware in time.
[2] Sundbärg notes the interesting fact that in Sweden in recent years this ratio has been highest in those counties where emigration has been particularly heavy.

ditions in our country leave much to be desired, as appears from the distribution by marital status which shows that in 1906, 201,000 out of 216,000 men in the group 20–25 were unmarried, of the 194,000 in the 25–30 group 119,000 were bachelors or widowers, and of 168,000 in the group 30–35 there were 62,000 who were not married.

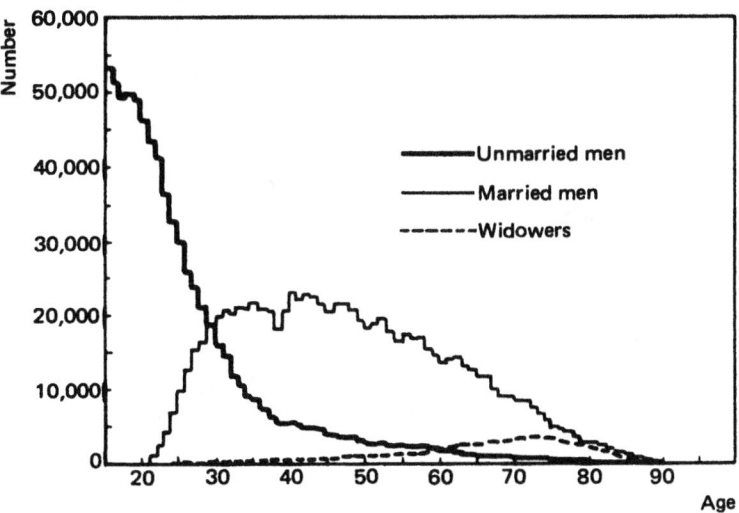

Fig. 5. Distribution of marital status in 1906, men.

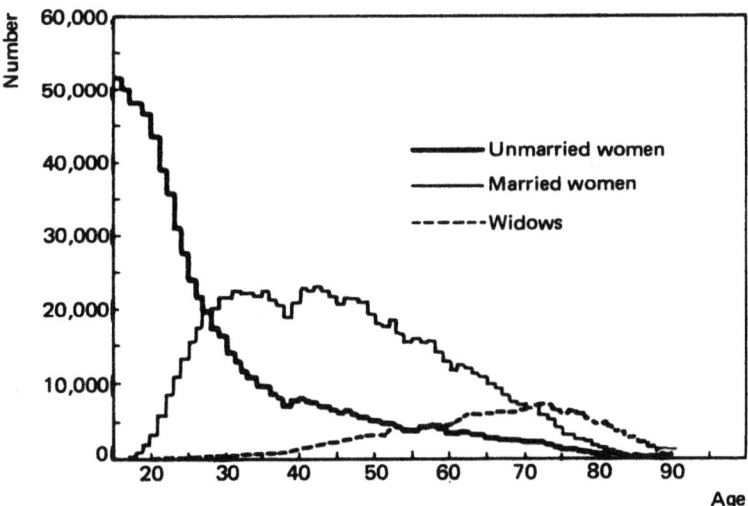

Fig. 6. Distribution of marital status in 1906, women.

The corresponding figures for women were in ages 20–25, 177,000 spinsters out of 219,000, in 25–30, 100,000 spinsters and 1600 widows out of 196,000 and in 30–35, 59,400 spinsters and 3300 widows in a total of 173,000. In the next five-year bracket, 35–40, the number of never-married women was 41,400 and the number of widows 5200 while the number of never-married men and widowers was only 36,000. In this age group the excess of the female population sharply reduces the marriage frequency. See also Figs. 5 and 6. Among the many unfavourable consequences of the low frequency of marriage, we shall encounter one already in the following section.

III
The Changes in Population. Mortality

Changes in the size and composition of a population are easily seen to depend on four factors: fertility, mortality, immigration and emigration. Of these I shall first treat the second, or mortality. It is true that death is the terminal point of the life of an individual, but in the life of the peoples, mortality is the most important aspect of turnover, and thereby of life; it is mortality that makes the other changes possible and necessary and puts its stamp on the actual composition of the population. It is well known that mortality is everywhere high in the first year of life; however, very great differences prevail. Along with Norway, Sweden is nowadays in the lead with a comparatively low infant mortality (less than 9 per cent of live births); possibly Ireland has even lower figures but her statistical records are not considered particularly reliable. On the other hand, infant mortality is very high ($2\frac{1}{2}$–3 times higher than in Sweden) in Germany, particularly the southern parts, in Austria, and in Russia.[1] There are also very great differences between different regions of the same country. In Sweden, mortality in the first year of life was on the whole unusually low in 1906, and it varied between 56.4 per thousand in the County of Värmland and 114.2 per thousand in the County of Norrbotten. In the city of Stockholm it was only 107.6 per thousand. In the preceding decade these mortality rates were 70.2, 130.1, and 152.3 per thousand respectively. There are also great differences between social classes. The rich have everywhere low infant mortality, to some extent—by the recourse to wet-nurses—at the direct expense of the poor. A few years ago, infant mortality in the city of Erfurt was 30.5 per cent in the working class, 17.3 per cent in the middle class, and 8.9 per cent among the upper classes. A similar difference is observed between legitimate and illegitimate children.

That inadequate *care* of the children is the most important reason for these differences is shown by some figures presented by the French doctor Monod

---

[1] Infant mortality in Cologne was in a few years reported to be as high as 695 per thousand; possibly exceptional circumstances such as abandoned children, etc., may have contributed.

in *Archiv für soziale Gesetzgebung*, 1888. According to him, mortality in the first year of life in Château-Chinon, near Paris, which supplied many wet-nurses, was regularly 33 per cent, but during the occupation of Paris, when the wet-nurses had to stay at home, it was only 17 per cent. The same locality also receives a great number of abandoned infants from Paris. Some of these were completely without supervision, another part was inspected three times a year at the expense of the local authority, and another part enjoyed the care of a benevolent society and was perpetually supervised. In the first of these groups, i.e. the unsupervised children, mortality reached 71 per cent; in the second group it was only 26 per cent, and in the third group it was 12 per cent—a striking demonstration of the old saying that high mortality among children is the reflection "not of the natural order, but of the social disorder".

After the first year, mortality rates decline rapidly and for both boys and girls it reaches its minimum in the ages 10–15 (less than 4 per thousand, and in 1906 even less than 3 per thousand for boys), whereupon it increases steadily but, in favourable conditions (married men in rural Sweden), very slowly. Until very recently great discrepancies have prevailed between rural and urban populations (the cities still show higher mortality among men but lower among women; on average, however, rural and urban mortality is nowadays roughly equal) as well as between married and unmarried men, both rural and urban. Unmarried men show consistently higher mortality. In Sweden the difference is observed from the age of 19. Between 20 and 45, mortality of unmarried men is almost twice as high as among married ones. One is inclined to suspect a source of error: one might imagine younger married men to constitute a select class of physically strong or economically favoured individuals, and conversely one might suspect the unmarried men in older age groups to constitute a reject class of weaker individuals. However, this objection is refuted, or at least weakened, by the fact that the widowers in the various age brackets have about the same high mortality as the unmarried men. It is remarkable that the mortality of married men of 20–25 is about as low as among boys in the age group 10–15, which represents the minimum.

For women over 25, the same thing holds true, but in a much lesser degree. In the younger age groups, on the other hand, the mortality among married women is even higher than among unmarried ones, clearly due to the risks associated with childbirth and its numerous attendant diseases, although the progress of aseptic practices has considerably reduced these dangers in recent years. For men, however, marriage can literally be termed a vital condition.

Occupational diseases do not play nearly the part in mortality that is very often claimed, although certainly some occupations are directly hazardous to health. What is important, however, is whether the occupation is rural or urban, if marriage is frequent or rare, etc., in other words the general causes of high or low mortality that we have just mentioned.

As for the impact of economic conditions on mortality, studies by, among others, the Danish doctor Th. Sörensen have showed that, as expected, there is a considerable excess mortality among the poor, especially in the ages over 35. However, his investigation only concerns the citizens of Copenhagen, and it seems that in the countryside, at least in Sweden, mortality is rather low even among people living in very plain but hygienic conditions.

Average mortality has declined rapidly in Sweden in the last century. In the second half of the eighteenth century, it was 27 per thousand; at present it is usually not even 16 per thousand and in 1906 it was insignificantly more than 14 per thousand. The improvement has not only benefited the infants, which is a common misconception, but also and even to a greater extent the higher age groups. The same thing has happened in other countries, particularly in the last quarter of the century. No small part of this should be attributed to the sanitary improvements in the cities (where mortality used to be much higher than in the countryside) as the result of piped water and effective sewage, but sanitary and economic conditions for the population as a whole have also improved. However, the evidence cited here shows how much further mortality could be brought down, even in Sweden, by healthier and more natural ways of life, higher nuptiality, and improved child care. We shall return to a necessary condition for all such improvements and then also say something about mortality in the past, so far as it is known.

IV
Fertility

The vacancies which death incessantly occasions in the ranks of the population are primarily filled by the advance of the younger and more numerous age brackets, and ultimately by fertility. The maintenance of the population is thus the first and most obvious function of fertility, and this is enough to show how closely it must be related to the level of mortality. This task is also incomparably the most important one that new births have to fill: the increase of the species, which is often mentioned alongside it or even given priority, is as we shall see entirely secondary, subordinate, and temporary in nature.

As is well known, there are considerable fertility differentials among countries. In Eastern Europe, fertility is extremely high, in France it is very low, and also in Ireland and in the eastern states of the USA. But there are also great differences among various parts of the same country: in the Swedish county of Norrbotten the crude birth rate in the decade 1896–1905 was close to 39 per thousand, on the island of Gotland it was not quite 21 per thousand, approximately the present level in France. Other parts of Sweden also show low birth rates, e.g. Skaraborg with 21.6 and Älvsborg with 22.8 per thousand in 1906.

The national average in that year was 25.7 per thousand, but it would have been much lower if the northern counties, particularly the two extreme ones, had not been characterized by a fertility more appropriate to colonial countries than to areas which in fact cannot support their own population, let alone make room for any immigration from the rest of the country. This is why Sweden still has a birth rate which by a good one-third exceeds the number of 100,000 new births a year although this, as we have seen, would be enough to maintain the present population.

The level of fertility in our society is primarily determined by the number of married women in fertile ages (in which one might include the group between 17 and 47). Unmarried women also bear children but far more rarely; on the average only about one-eighth as many. This is why a drop in the birth rate may be due entirely to reduced nuptiality, without any decline in marital fertility. This has also been the case in Sweden until quite recently. It is only in the last decades that there has been a decline of fertility within marriage, especially in the case of higher age groups of women.

In those cases where the birth records make it possible to distinguish between families of different wealth, as in different parts of the same city, fertility is consistently found to be lower among the rich than among the poor. The careful investigations of Westergaard and Rubin concerning the population of Copenhagen confirm this, at least in essence.[1] On the other hand, the American Frank Fetter (*Das Bevölkerungsgesetz*, Halle, 1893) has tried to prove that this phenomenon is fairly recent, at least in the case of America. There, the wealthier classes used to have numerous children but now have very few, and the same seems to have been the case in other countries as well. As the poor generally adopt and imitate the custom of the rich, one ought, like Leroy-Beaulieu, to anticipate a gradual reduction of fertility in the entire civilized world, such as has been going on in France for a century now.[2] We shall try to demonstrate in the following that such a reduction is actually an imperative necessity.

---

[1] It is nevertheless remarkable that according to this investigation the lowest fertility is not found among the prosperous classes, but among accountants, lower civil servants, and similar groups, while higher civil servants, merchants and capitalists have a fertility somewhere between the previous classes and the working class. From this it appears that the lower fertility of the wealthy is not, as we are sometimes told, directly and physically related to their favourable economic conditions, but at least largely a result of their greater prudence, responsibility and foresight.

A particularly interesting piece of statistical information in this connection has been provided by the large English society for self-help called Hearts of Oak. In this society, the members of which are chiefly well-paid workers or lesser clerks, an allowance of 30 shillings a week is paid while a wife of a member is in bed after childbirth. It now appears that since about 1880 the percentage of such allowances has incessantly declined and that at present it is less than half of what it was 30 years ago. It is true that the average age of the members has increased somewhat, but this can only slightly have contributed to the change in question, which indubitably suggests that there has been a major change in attitudes and social habits among the elite of the English working class.

[2] *Traité d'économie politique*, 2nd ed., Vol. IV, pp. 473 et seq.
Cf. Sundbärg, *Bevölkerungsstatistik Schwedens*, pp. 47 et seq.

The question of illegitimate children deserves special attention on account of its great social significance. It would be wrong to imagine that births out of wedlock are generally the fruit of moral depravation and frivolity. Were this the case, one would expect such births in younger years, before the character has been sufficiently stabilized. It is true that unmarried mothers are generally younger than married ones, but this is entirely due to the fact that there are so few married women in the younger age brackets. If one considers the numbers of married and unmarried mothers in relation to the number of married and unmarried women in the various age brackets, it turns out that the relation is the opposite one. Among married women fertility is highest in the younger age groups; among unmarried women, on the other hand, there are fairly few mothers under 20, and then the ratio increases and reaches a maximum at 25–30. Thereupon it again decreases, although rather slowly so that even at the age of 40 the fertility rate of unmarried women until a few years ago was higher than at the age of 19. Undoubtedly this is generally due to a natural maternal or sexual instinct which in younger years is held back by various social considerations.

Genuine moral depravity (prostitution) is a very different matter and seems to be initiated at very young ages. On the other hand, illegitimate children generally suffer from inadequate care and are subject to many unfavourable influences, and thus become a threat to society, the most suspect classes of which, such as criminals and prostitutes, are in no small measure recruited from their ranks, although as the statistics show, not nearly so frequently as one very often imagines. Steps to remedy this inconvenience are highly desirable, but no conceivable measures could be as efficient as the promotion of early marriage for both men and women. There is one objection against this, namely that an increased birth rate and population would *a priori* seem to be a necessary consequence of such measures, and we shall now consider this problem.[1]

---

[1] Lately there has been a remarkable change in extramarital fertility. The number of births to unmarried women in the higher age groups has shown a significant reduction but those in younger age groups, 15–25, an even stronger increase. There is no reason to hesitate about the explanation of the first of those changes. It is found among married women as well, not only in our own but in all countries, and is no doubt due to the increasing prevalence of voluntary sterility (the use of means to prevent conception). As to the second change, its causes might well deserve closer investigation. If I am not mistaken, it is at least in great measure a matter of quite regular unions, in other words marriages—though without legal ceremonies—entered into at an early age in the industrial working class. As it offsets the sharp drop in the marriage ratio and serves as protection against prostitution, this phenomenon is in itself, in my view, to be welcomed, although it would be even better if parenthood in those early unions were postponed a few years, until the parents were economically, and probably often also physically, better capable of assuming its obligations. In any case the traditional statistical categories of "legitimate" and "illegitimate" children, and "married" vs. "unmarried" mothers no longer seem fully to correspond to the social conditions which they were originally intended to describe.

V
The Natural Increase of Population

The excess of births over deaths—if there is one—is called the natural increase in a country, to distinguish it from the actual one which is also affected by migration. If the annual birth rate is 26 per thousand and the death rate 16 per thousand, which has been the case in Sweden in recent years, more or less, the rate of natural increase is 10 per thousand or 1 per cent a year. To estimate the growth during a longer period one must resort to compound interest It then turns out that an annual growth of 1 per cent means a doubling of the population in 70 years; a rate of growth of 0.7 per cent yields a doubling period of almost exactly 100 years; if the natural rate of increase is only 0.7 per thousand the population doubles only in almost 1000 years. On the other hand, an annual increase of 28 per thousand would double the population in 25 years, and a rate of growth of about 47 per thousand would mean a doubling after only 15 years, etc.

There has been much argument about whether such rapid rates of growth as indicated by the last examples would be physiologically possible, as Malthus claimed in his day. That it can only occur quite exceptionally is self-evident, but that is not the issue. To show that in exceptionally favourable external circumstances such growth was conceivable, Malthus cited the American population in the eighteenth century, but these figures are of course highly uncertain, and the same is true of the statistics from newer colonial territories, such as New Zealand and Australia, where it is difficult to distinguish the natural increase from the effect of the simultaneous immigration. To find direct evidence in the statistical records of older countries is hopeless; however, it might be possible to find it confirmed by indirect means in European statistics. The necessary conditions—sufficiently high birth rates and sufficiently low death rates—are actually found in contemporary Europe, although not combined in one and the same place. The extreme birth and death rates recorded are a birth rate of 55 per thousand in eastern Russia and a death rate of 15 per thousand or even less in certain parts of Sweden. The difference is no less than 40 per thousand or 4 per cent, which corresponds to a doubling period between 17–18 years. This would seem to prove that such an incredibly rapid rate of growth of population is physically or physiologically possible, for if those birth and death rates can exist in separation, there is no reason why they should not, in sufficiently favourable external conditions, be combined simultaneously in one and the same country.

If each married couple on average had four grown children, who themselves married and had as many children, the population would double in the course of each generation, but against this well-known argument Rumelin (*Schönbergs Handbuch*, "Die Bevölkerungslehre") objects that it would only double certain age groups of the population but not the population as a whole. Similarly, the Danish economist E. Meyer argues in the article on population in Salomonsen's dictionary that a continued doubling of the population every 25 years or less would be unthinkable, as the youngest age groups would become too numerous compared with the older ones, so that the women in fertile ages would not suffice to produce the necessary fertility. All this is due to a misunderstanding. If every woman bears on average four children between her twentieth and thirtieth year, and then no more—which is no exaggerated rate of fertility— the age group of 0–1 will be about four times as numerous as one annual cohort of women in the age of 25 or 26, and thus twice as numerous as an annual cohort of both sexes of that age. If health conditions are so favourable that deaths only occur in the upper age brackets, these circumstances must necessarily imply an organic doubling of the population, i.e. of all its age groups, every 25 years. If one similarly imagines that women in fertile ages, on both sides of their thirtieth year, bore on average eight living children each—which is not beyond the realm of the possible—the population would increase four times in about thirty years and thus double in fifteen. This is clearly not inconceivable.

If we compare this physiologically possible or conceivable rate of growth with the actual one, the differences are stark. We must not be misled by the great increase of population which in the nineteenth century occurred in Europe, North America and many other parts of the world which were settled by Europeans or controlled by them, such as the East Indies, Java, etc. This must be considered as a purely exceptional case, dependent on the rare combination of favourable economic circumstances which arose when European agriculture, which had been carried on in much the same manner ever since Charlemagne was thoroughly revolutionized at the end of the eighteenth century, and when we started to draw on the enormous—though not inexhaustible —energy resources from ancient geological eras which have been preserved in our coal deposits. Even France, which is usually cited as an instance of a stationary country, has in the recent decade increased its population both absolutely and relatively more than in any preceding period. A stationary population—or rather alternating increases and decreases, resulting in a very slow growth— has at all times and in all countries been the principal demographic rule and we must imagine it to remain so even in the future.

If we consider mankind as a whole, e.g. during the last six millenia, it certainly numbered more than 100 million at the beginning of this period, but some parts of the world, such as Egypt, had already reached a significant degree of civilization. At the present time it is estimated to be about 1600 million or slightly more: it would thus have doubled four times, or on the average once every 1500 years. Looking forward, we can only say that even such a slow rate of growth must ultimately exceed the limits of the possible. It is against the background of this striking conflict between the physiologically and the actually (economically) possible that the issue of population must be seen if its overwhelming social and economic significance, which overshadows all other issues, is to be apparent.

VI
Immigration and Emigration

Even the migrations, which have played and continue to play such an important part in present-day population statistics, naturally only constitute episodes in the lives of human populations. The emigration of our days has primarily flowed from Europe to North America, and in a lesser degree to South America and Australia. Relatively speaking, it has been largest from Ireland, where the population, chiefly for this reason, has declined to slightly more than half of what it was in the 1840s, a phenomenon which is so far unique in modern European statistics. But emigration has been significant also from England and Germany, and lately from Italy, Austria, and Russia. The Scandinavian countries have also had significant emigration in comparison to their population: from Sweden it began on a major scale only after the distressed years of 1867–68, and continued during the whole of the 1880s and the beginning of the 1890s. In the thirty years between 1868 and 1897, over 660,000 people emigrated from Sweden alone to the United States, and for a while one could estimate that of those children born in Sweden who would reach grown-up age, every third one would finish his days as an American. Beginning in 1894, a considerable reduction occurred, partly because conditions had improved at home, to some extent as a consequence of the previous emigration, but also because of the natural or legal obstacles which were raised in the United States against continued immigration. The emigration of women seems to be more stable than that of men, so that in years of low overall emigration, female emigration, and particularly net female emigration, has sometimes come to exceed male emigration.

Another kind of migration is also very important from a demographic and economic point of view, i.e. the migration from the country to the city. The rural population in Sweden is growing very slowly or not at all, and the agricultural population has even declined in the last 20 or 30 years, a consequence of the mechanization of agriculture, among other things.[1] The population of the cities, on the other hand, has increased rapidly. The main cause here, as in other countries, is the rapid development of the transport system. The congregation

---

[1] In 1870, the Swedish population in agriculture and fishing was 2,996,000, but in 1906 it was only 2,681,000. As a share of the total population it had dropped from 71.87 to 50.23 per cent. At the same time the population in industry and mining increased from 673,000 to 1,683,000, or from 14.71 to 31.54 per cent, and that in commerce and transportation from 211,000 to 618,000, or from 5 to 11.58 per cent. See also Fig. 7.

of the population in the cities favours the division of labour and results in economic advantages, which are at a certain point offset by the difficulty of procuring food and other necessities from remoter areas and marketing the city's produce. This difficulty, however, is reduced by improved transportation: railroads, canals, steamships. Thereby the advantages of concentration will again offset the inconveniences—especially so far as the major cities are concerned—and an increase of urban population at the expense of the countryside can once again take place before the economic conditions offered to immigrants again decline to the rural level.

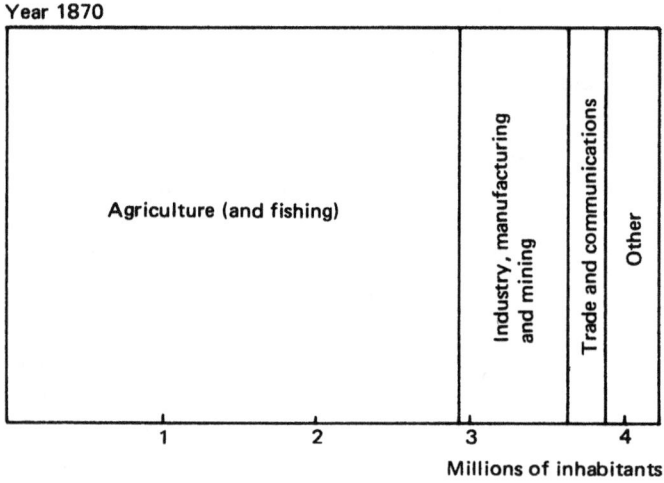

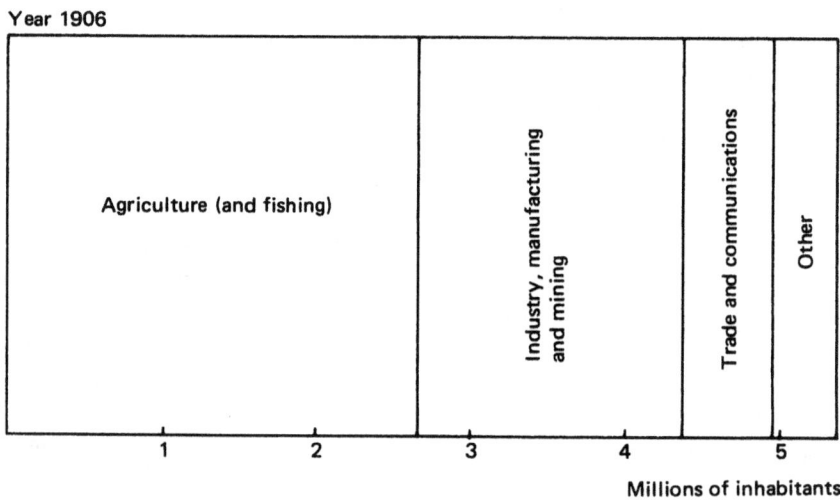

Fig. 7. Occupational distribution in Sweden.

It is easily realized that from a demographic point of view, neither the one nor the other kind of migration can have more than transitory significance. North America, at least the USA, is now fully colonized and thereby fully settled, if not by European then at least by American yardsticks. In the course of the last few decades, the settlement of North America has, as R. Giffen points out, roughly meant that the north-south frontier, separating the colonized territory from the uninhabited prairie, was each year moved several miles westward. Once this line reached the Rocky Mountains it could not advance much further, and for the possibly considerable but nevertheless much slower increase of population for which there might still be room in the United States, the country's own natural increase will therefore soon be more than adequate. The same is true of the migration from the country to the cities. Even if all industry were concentrated in the cities, which for natural reasons cannot or will not be the case, and is not the case in our country, then at least industry and agriculture must be balanced—a country cannot be exclusively or even predominantly industrial, unless there are other countries which almost lack industry and only devote themselves to agriculture, a condition which is increasingly rare as the colonial countries' populations grow.

VII
The Malthusian Theory of Population

History

It might seem that such a simple and obvious matter as the natural inclination of population to outpace food supplies ought to have attracted attention from very early times. But in the absence of any scientifically designed statistics it was not so easy to demonstrate this tendency, nor to discover the proper relationship of cause and effect. The extreme mortalities, which time and time again wiped out large numbers in plagues, wars, and famine, could rather be seen to call for all the fertile powers of the species to make up for the voids. In many of the customary rites of antiquity, barbarous like the time itself—human sacrifice, infanticide, etc.—one may distinguish a tendency to restrict population, but probably it was rarely a conscious one.[1]

In small and closed societies, especially those which had already reached a high level of civilization, as the Greek republics, the necessity of limiting population must nevertheless have made itself felt very starkly. We find both Plato, in his youthful work on the State, and Aristotle, his disciple, formulate specific requirements in this regard and propose far-reaching restrictions on

---

[1] According to Aristotle, King Minos deliberately introduced certain sexual aberrations to Crete in order to prevent overpopulation, but it is useless to speculate about whether this is more than an anecdote.

nuptiality and, in emergencies, abortion and even infanticide.[1] In the Middle Ages also we encounter such more or less conscious restrictions. Monastic life was in itself one of these, and even the advantages of the two-child system seem to have been familiar, judging from the medieval expression *oskebarn* (desired children) to describe a son and a daughter. However, the high infant mortality and the incessant epidemics during the Middle Ages and well into the modern age seem to have obscured this insight for most people, not only in the population at large but also its thinkers and teachers, and made any restraint seem superfluous. The most appalling of these epidemics was the Black Death in the middle of the fourteenth century, which for quite some time brought a sharp reduction of population but also considerably improved the position of the working classes.

The following figures, cited from von Inama-Sternegg, may serve to illustrate characteristic demographic conditions in earlier times. The first concern the canton of Zurich in Switzerland and are based on the tax ledgers:

Year	Population (approx.)
1467	50,000
1564	65,658
1610	140,000
1634	79,373
1771	118,000

To explain these curious fluctuations, Inama says Zurich was struck by plague in the years 1482, 1493, 1502, 1519, 1541, 1564, 1575, 1582, 1586, 1595, 1611 and 1628. In the seventeenth century we must also allow for some effects of the Thirty Years' War. The latter is particularly apparent in the case of the population of Wurtemberg, which has been derived from clergy's lists of the number of communicants, to which $\frac{1}{6}$ has been added for non-communicants. Already

Year	Population	Year	Population
1622	444,552	1673	251,835
1634	414,536	1679	264,616
1639	97,258 (!)	1750	467,132
1645	121,106	1754	477,112
1652	166,014	1759	478,979
1669	218,455		

in the beginning of this series one can trace the effects of the war, which in 1634 was in its seventeenth year. But it was only after 1634 that the catastrophe

---

[1] Of course these ancient philosophers should not be taken to have been convinced Malthusians in the modern sense. The limitation they advocated primarily applied to the full citizens and was meant to facilitate the political organization characteristic of the small Greek republics. Cf. L. v. Bortkiewicz in *Tübinger Zeitschrift*, 1906, pp. 383 ff. But B. is probably going too far when he refuses to attribute to them any interest whatever in restraining population. To extinguish human lives or their embryos on the strength of a merely political idea would hardly have occurred to men such as Plato and Aristotle unless it seemed urgently necessary.

occurred which the demographic result lets us imagine: the population dropped to less than ¼ in only five years. It was to take about a century for the population to increase fourfold again, and we can probably take it for granted that during this time any thought of restraining population growth would have been rejected by most people as unreasonable. One was probably more than ever inclined to abide by Luther's injunction that all men should marry at 20, and all women between 15 and 18—and let the heavenly powers provide for the children.

This attitude survives even in our day, but in the second half of the eighteenth century a more rational attitude began to spread among the educated classes. Justus Möser (1720–94) is, in his *Patriotische Phantasien* clearly a German forerunner to Malthus. In his "Letter to a Young Matron" who has asked him whether she should have her children inoculated against smallpox in spite of the risk—cowpox vaccination had not yet been discovered—he ironically objects to the doctor's attempt to prevent the useful and necessary weeding-out of the population by disease. In the old days, he says, it was considered a law of nature that half of all children must die before the age of ten; a pious matron was pleased and contented if the Lord only took an even share from her, or even if he took one child more or so. In the future, after smallpox and other scourges have been wiped out by the advance of the medical arts, she would either have to breastfeed her children herself (as women are generally considered less likely to become pregnant during the suckling period) or else she must stop bearing children from the age of 20. (This last addition is an interesting proof of the extremely early age of marriage that prevailed among the prosperous classes.) He compares the medical efforts to fight epidemics with the attempt of a hangman to resuscitate a thief who has hanged himself in jail in order to be able to hang him more formally the following day. With a sense of humour which must strike us as rather gross, Möser says that if it were only a matter of the lower classes the damage would not be serious, as they can always be placed in front of the cannon and shot at; the proliferation of the upper classes could not so easily be undone, etc.

The great economists Turgot and Adam Smith were more direct forerunners of Malthus. Especially in Smith's work we find the outline of the Malthusian theory of population clearly enunciated. Smith says that each species will naturally increase to the limit of its means of subsistence and that no species can possibly increase beyond it. But among human beings it is in civilized societies only in the lower classes that the lack of subsistence directly limits the further increase of the species, and this cannot be done except by the destruction of many of the children produced in their marriages. In the Highlands of Scotland it was not uncommon, he says, for a woman to have borne twenty children but not even have two of them left. When high wages temporarily occur, the labourers are enabled to keep more children alive, but this satiates the labour market and makes a new reduction necessary. In this manner, he concludes, the demand for people will necessarily regulate their production[1] as in the case of any other commodity—accelerate it when it is too slow, and check it when it is too quick. This demand regulates the increase of population in all the countries of the world and makes for rapid increase in North America, slow and stepwise growth in Europe, and no increase at all in China. (*Wealth of Nations*, Book I, Ch. 8.)

This is the whole theory of population in a nutshell, although applied only to the poor; it is what we would in modern terminology call the iron law of wages for the working class. Malthus' chief work, *The Principle of Population*, was in its first edition of 1798 only a pamphlet, which was largely based on Smith. Karl Marx called it "von Ende zum anderen ein vordeklamiertes Plagiat". It might have been more correct to call it a compilation, for in his preface Malthus expressly indicated his sources. The second and following editions, however, constituted an entirely new work and presented a rich body of evidence, based on extensive reading and his own observations. Yet it was the first edition, perhaps principally the first edition, that attracted most attention, although nobody had attached particular significance to Adam Smith's basically quite similar conclusions. Why was this ?

The explanation is undoubtedly that the times had changed. Smith's book was published in 1776 and Malthus' in 1798—they were separated by the historic event we call the French Revolution, with all its social consequences. That the lower classes lived in great poverty was in the *ancien régime* taken for granted or even considered a beneficent and providential arrangement for the good of "society", i.e. for the upper classes. A scientific explanation of the causes of such a state of affairs was therefore primarily of theoretical and Platonic interest. But the French Revolution made the equality of all—economic as well as otherwise—and a radical improvement of the conditions of the poor into a practical claim, rather than a philosophical or philanthropic dream. Its most devoted followers, such as the Englishman Godwin, of whom Malthus' own father was a great admirer, held that this claim had only to be formulated in order to be realized: if only all social barriers were removed, they thought general prosperity would emerge by itself. It was to these exaggerated expectations that Malthus primarily objected. His book was a cold shower directed against the revolutionary enthusiasts, and some hailed it as the gospel of conservatism, others as inhuman and hostile to labour. Both views were equally shortsighted. Of course, Malthus is conservative in the sense that—whether correctly or incorrectly is another matter—he tried to demonstrate a rational basis and a higher purpose behind the existing arrangements of society, which by him were seen as in present circumstances necessary barriers against an excessive increase in population. On the other hand, unlike all earlier economists

---

[1] Von Möser had already used the very same expression, apologizing for its crudeness.

—even Adam Smith cannot be entirely excepted—he for the first time posited the welfare of the masses and the labouring classes as the highest goal of social evolution and also indicated to the workers the only fully effective road to this goal, or at any rate an indispensable precondition for it. From Malthus on, one may assert, economics does not see the worker merely as a means to the realization of the objectives of other classes, but as an end in himself. All this is particularly true of the later editions of his work, which constitute a far more extensive and in a genuine sense scientific work. In those, Malthus moderated some of his too pessimistic conclusions: "moral restraint" was expressly said to be a check of population, alongside the "positive" checks of war, pestilence, and famine. He also removed certain theological arguments of dubious value and finally added a wealth of historic and statistical information, collected in the course of many years of travel and studies, e.g. in the Scandinavian countries, in order to illustrate the working of the Law of Population in various countries and at various times.

The Malthusian Series

The briefest, and at any rate most familiar, expression of Malthus' theory which occurred already in the first edition and which he did not apparently have the heart to strike out, is the comparison of the two series. He says that mankind has a natural tendency to grow in geometric progression, i.e. as the numbers 1, 2, 4, 8, 16, 32, etc.; but food supplies could at most increase in arithmetic progression, as the numbers 1, 2, 3, 4, 5, 6, etc. The colossal and increasing discrepancy between these series was meant to illustrate the difference which we have already mentioned between the physiological and actual potential for increase. As for the first of these series, the geometric one, it may be said to be quite correct, even self-evident, for as long as the human constitution is basically unchanged, the time which is adequate for a first doubling of the population must also suffice for another doubling, and then yet another, etc. The trouble is only that the higher numbers, which are only intended to bring out the unreasonableness of an unchecked population growth and could thus never occur in reality, are easily confused by superficial minds with a kind of prophecy about the future size of mankind, which they are of course least of all intended to be.

The arithmetic series again is more in the nature of a loose speculation. It is really only based on the impossibility of a geometric growth of food supplies and is basically only a disguise for this self-evident fact. The laws which actually govern the growth of supplies of food and other means of subsistence in a country are the subject of study of the theory of production and especially agricultural economics. However, experience shows that this growth is highly irregular. Occasionally, as in the last two centuries, it may be very rapid for some considerable time, but generally it is very slow. It is not rare for it to cease entirely over long periods so that production is stationary. Rumelin suggests that the

Roman farmer in our days probably does not reap either more or less per "jugerum" than in the days of Cincinnatus. Production may also decline, as is often the case and must ultimately become the case in the so-called extractive industries, e.g. mining, or in excessive forestry which does not allow for natural replacement, or in irrational agriculture which does not restore the nutrients to the earth.

The Core of Malthus' Doctrine
The most important element is neither the arithmetic nor the geometric series but the growth factor of the latter, the annual percentage rate of growth—or, which is the same thing, the time in which the population would double under favourable external circumstances. As we have already mentioned, Malthus claimed that this was at most 25 years, corresponding to an annual increase of nearly 3 per cent. We have already tried to show that this claim was by no means an exaggeration. Once this is conceded, all the rest basically follows by a simple proof of unreasonableness, for it is quite self-evident that the growth of the means of subsistence cannot in the long run proceed at this or an at all comparable rate. Curiously, many of Malthus' followers, especially in recent times, have overlooked or rather intentionally left out this important point. They believe themselves to have countered the attack of the opponents by making the point that even if the physiologically possible growth were much slower than Malthus assumed, and would only double the population in 50 or 100 years, it would nevertheless in the fullness of time exceed all limits. By diluting, as it were, Malthus' pointed proposition, one does him a disservice. Practically speaking, the situation would be quite different if the natural tendency for population growth were so slow that a doubling would not occur in less than 100, 200, or 500 years (which was thought to be the actual rate of growth in Adam Smith's days). The fertility reduction required to turn such slow growth into complete stability would be fairly insignificant and would probably occur by itself, in case of need, without becoming a troublesome issue of social policy. But when, as is actually the case, only a small fraction of the physiological potential of population growth can be realized, the matter is different, and it follows that counteracting forces of great power, and thus of the greatest social significance, must always be active in order to check the tendency to multiply.

The Checks to Population
Malthus' work is basically devoted to these checks and their effects at different times and in different countries. They are necessarily of two kinds: preventive checks which reduce fertility, and repressive or positive ones which increase mortality. Among the former are late marriages, marital restraint and extra-marital abstinence, prostitution which signally reduces fertility, and finally

the so-called means of contraception of which there has recently been much talk and which aim to prevent conception. In the second category we have, on the one hand, the checks of nature itself, pestilence and hunger, and disease in general, especially among infants, and also those which more or less consciously are used by mankind itself, abortion and infanticide, vices that shorten life, e.g. alcoholism, and finally wars. But war, which used to be one of the principal positive checks to excessive population growth, has in our day taken on a different character. Modern wars and their prerequisite and consequence, the armed peace, are neither preventive nor positive checks in any real sense, but like diminishing productivity of the earth they contribute to a reduction of the otherwise available means of subsistence. They thereby reduce the welfare of population and thus indirectly its growth. The direct reduction of populations wrought by modern wars is of negligible importance.

The Malthusian Dilemma and Objections to his Doctrine
It is between these two kinds of checks, possibly between the different checks in the two categories, that mankind has to make its choice. This is the so-called Malthusian dilemma to which we shall soon return.

Malthus' doctrine has during the whole century been violently opposed both by scholars and laymen and by writers of the most varied political persuasions, from the defendants of the traditional social order and religion to extreme socialists. Through an irony of fate, economic development has also throughout this century seemed to constitute a forceful refutation of Malthus' predictions, for in spite of the fact that population has increased faster than in almost any preceding era, prosperity in Europe and elsewhere in the world has by no means been reduced but has, on the contrary, on the whole increased. But this can only in a superficial judgment shake the theoretical proof or the practical significance of Malthus' theses. Many of the objections levelled against his teaching actually have very little to do with science, and among living economists there are probably few who do not agree with Adolf Wagner's conclusion after a thorough presentation of the theory of population in the third edition of his *Grundlegung:* "Robert Malthus behält somit in allem wesentlichen Recht." ("Thus Malthus remains correct in all that is essential.")

But little is gained by such general agreement. The difficulties begin when one tries to draw more practical conclusions for action in the present circumstances. In the final section, we shall try to indicate how this is to be done.

VIII
The Two Population Problems

A closer study of the population problem leads to the conclusion that it actually consists of two problems of essentially different nature which ought conceptually to be kept apart even if they are in many ways closely related. The confusion of these two questions in one single discussion has given the battles raging over population the impassioned and sterile character which easily occurs when the two sides are not fully agreed about the nature of the issue. One of these questions could be stated as follows: which is, under given conditions, the optimal density of population in a country ? Is the actual population under these conditions too large, about right, or too small, and which criteria could be used ?

This is clearly an eminently economic question even though perhaps other than purely economic considerations may be pertinent to its solution. To be able to treat it exhaustively one ought therefore to be informed of all those economic conditions that are related to the density of population, and this means nearly all economic phenomena. It is not even to be excluded that the reply may to some extent differ depending upon whether one economic system or another is taken as a point of departure, either a modern individualistic system or a more or less collectivist one. In one word: the reply to this question does not belong to the introduction but to the conclusion of an economic analysis and is to be regarded as one of its most important results.[1] It is obvious that the question is in itself of the greatest theoretical and practical importance; it is all the more striking that hardly a single economist has devoted himself to it in depth. There have been fairly meaningless disputes concerning the existence or non-existence of so-called overpopulation, i.e. a condition in which a country has more inhabitants than it can feed, and it has been overlooked that the most important question does not concern the possible maximum population but the optimal one, the point where an increase of population would no longer in itself lead to any average increase in welfare but to the opposite. For my own part, I have gradually reached the conviction that this optimum has already been considerably exceeded in our own country as in all countries of Europe, so that the road to increased prosperity does not lie in any further increase of population but rather in an energetic reduction of the population, continued through decades. (On this subject, see my report to the Commission on Emigration.) However strange such a thought may at first seem, it is nevertheless an almost self-evident conclusion as soon as one consistently embraces the general point of view of the Malthusian doctrine. Before population reaches the point where the lack of food becomes an absolute obstacle to further increase it must first have passed a stage—and at this stage presumably all old countries find themselves—where an increase in numbers is not entirely impossible but must nevertheless be paid for by a sacrifice either of prosperity already attained or of the improvements that technical progress would otherwise have rendered possible.

---

[1] I remind the reader that this little essay was originally written as the introduction to a large (unfortunately not yet completed) economic treatise.

Those who think otherwise and who unhesitatingly recommend an increase of population for our own, as well as for other countries, the faster the better, are generally distinguished more by the strength of their patriotic sentiment than by the logic of their reasoning. What is most common is that they confuse cause and effect. Any improvement of economic conditions usually results in population growth; the conclusion is then drawn that the increase in population is itself the cause of the prosperity, although a rule that holds anywhere else in the physical world is that an effect tends to counteract and partly offset its own cause.

Or else they claim (as Professor P. Fahlbeck) support in the partially correct proposition of economic theory according to which large-scale production is more profitable than small-scale production. What is then forgotten is that an increased scale of production requires that all factors of production, thus also that of nature, can be increased at pleasure or as needed, which is to some extent true of those industries whose raw materials are ready-made in the interior of the earth or on its surface: mining, metallurgical industry, and even, for shorter periods, forestry. However, it is not at all the case for the production of foodstuffs.

Or else they refer (as the prominent agricultural expert Dr. J. Leffler) to modern improvements of agricultural technology through which intensive agriculture has been able to multiply yields per hectare several times. But this argument is not decisive, as long as it cannot be shown that intensive agriculture also yields more per unit of labour than more extensive (but otherwise rationally managed) agriculture. If the opposite is true—which seems to be the case in reality—intensive agriculture is only a last resort to provide for an already existing, too numerous population, but in no way something in itself desirable. What we wish to achieve is after all not primarily intensively cultivated fields but happy people.

The fear which is sometimes expressed that a nation which has once begun to reduce its numbers would then by some kind of natural necessity continue on this road to the point of complete self-destruction can, I think, without any further ado be rejected as a phantom of the mind. If a larger number of births will ever seem desirable from the point of view of a whole nation, and thus not just from that of the ruling classes, society would stand to gain from the financial support of large families, and that in such circumstances the birth rate could reach any level no one will doubt unless he knows very little of human nature.

The second problem of population is the following: in what way should the equilibrium between births and deaths, if it is necessary or desirable, be achieved and maintained? This question is obviously of a different nature, and, unlike the first one, it touches on a great number of other social concerns than the purely economic ones. Whether a population is dense or sparse, numerous or scanty, it must in the fullness of time become stationary, and even when growth is possible or desirable it will, at least in countries of old culture, necessarily fall far short of the physiologically possible rate of growth. This is true even of the exceptionally strong increase of population in the last century, for although the population of Western Europe nearly doubled in the nineteenth century and that of Eastern Europe (Russia, Hungary, Galicia and the Balkan states) more than doubled, this is far from doubling every 25 years.

Moreover, everything suggests that the rate of growth of population in the twentieth century which has now started must be considerably smaller than in the preceding one. If one extrapolates on the basis of the rate of natural increase in the years 1870–80, as Philippovich (*Grundriss d. pol. Oekon.*) points out, the combined population in the following countries: Germany, Austria-Hungary, Great Britain and Ireland, France, Italy, Switzerland, Sweden and Norway, Denmark, The Netherlands, and Belgium—i.e. all of Western Europe plus Hungary and Galicia—which in 1890 amounted to 220 million would at the end of this century be 658 million. However, with the exception of Hungary not a single one of these countries can nowadays feed itself—at any rate they do not—and together they consume the combined surplus of grain and meat from the entire rest of the world. Philippovich says that the postulated rate of growth would mean that they would triple their demand for food imports. But this is clearly much too little; in spite of its size the present imports constitute only a smaller share—say, 20–30 per cent of the total food needs of Western Europe. If the population and the total need for food trebled, and if domestic production of food could not be correspondingly increased, which is not very likely, the need for foreign imports would increase much more. In the extreme case where the agriculture of Western Europe remained stationary, it would be 8–10 times as great as now. But those countries which are now the granaries of Europe—the United States, Russia, the East Indies, Australia, Argentina and Canada—do not themselves have stable populations. They are growing, and even at a far greater speed than Western Europe itself. Although the initial phase of colonization of a previously uninhabited country leads to an ever-increasing surplus of grain and meat, the condition will of course soon become the reverse. It is therefore only a matter of time, probably only a few decades, until these countries, particularly the first three, will themselves consume the totality of their present food surpluses and at the same time, as the result of their own industrial growth, essentially cease to be consumers of Western European manufactures.

That the growth of population, even when it is seen on a global scale, does not hold out the infinite prospects which many love to imagine, is fairly clear from a calculation by the Englishman Ravenstein. According to him, the total land area of the earth is estimated at about 120 million sq.km., of which 73 million, or about 140 times the surface of France, constitutes arable or relatively arable land. Another $36\frac{1}{2}$ million sq.km. are bare grasslands or steppes and almost 11 million sq.km. are waste land. Now, assuming that the first of these areas could be as densely settled as the central belt of Europe, from The Netherlands to the Black Sea, or by 60 inhabitants per sq.km. which is slightly less than the present density of France, and that prairie lands would be somewhat less settled, Ravenstein comes to the conclusion that in only about 180 years the total surface of the earth would be fully peopled, in as much as its total population would then be about 6 billion. All this is on the assumption that the present rate of natural increase, which he estimates at 8 per thousand for the globe as a whole, would be sustained. Leroy-Beaulieu cites these numbers, but in accordance with his general attitude he totally rejects all such "statistical phantasies", as he calls them, although he is obliged to concede that Ravenstein's estimates of the inhabitable and arable land surface of the globe rather overestimate than underestimate. Whatever the truth in this respect, the population of Europe will surely only in a very small measure be able to benefit from the space that the rest of the world might offer for another century or two. Already now, Europe ought practically speaking to be regarded as "au grand complet", to use Leroy-Beaulieu's expression.

A demographic stagnation, and perhaps even a decline, will therefore in all probability be the lot of Western Europe in the course of the present century and since, as we have seen, emigration is not likely to be able to accommodate the population surplus to any considerable degree, the question arises: how is the necessary restriction to be attained—by increased mortality or reduced fertility? It seems there can only be one reply: economists would probably be fairly unanimous on the latter alternative. Yet some voices are raised in defence of the former alternative of increased mortality. As among them we find a man of the stature of Charles Darwin, we must briefly comment on this position as well. Darwin himself relates that it was by the study of Malthus' work that he was led to postulate the principle of natural selection which after all is no more than "the principle of population extended to all of the animal and vegetable world". In *The Descent of Man* he raises a qualified objection to Malthus' own point of view: he argues that the repressive or positive check, whatever suffering it may inflict on humanity, cannot be completely set aside or even be significantly curtailed without a considerable danger that mankind would degenerate and decline.

The correct reply to this objection, which was never to my knowledge more closely elaborated by its originator, is probably that the so-called natural selection by its very nature is an unconscious selection and therefore ceases to exist, in its pure form, as soon as its significance has been discovered and realized. That a selection might be necessary even in the future is possible and even likely, but as Darwin himself suggested, it might take the form that the strongest or best-equipped individuals are given a primary responsibility for the propagation of the species. Whichever solution is chosen it will in any case no longer be a natural but a conscious and therefore more or less artificial selection. If one were to come to the conclusion that we should continue to produce more individuals than we can rear and then let "nature", i.e. hunger and disease, take care of the natural weeding-out, it must be in the full conviction that this method is among all possible ones better suited to the purpose and more appropriate than any other, which seems to be too great a claim, at any rate as long as no other methods have yet been tried.[1]

So far, we must then turn to the second group of measures: preventive measures against an excessive population increase. But which among them? Strictly speaking this is no longer an economic question, but its general social significance is so great that an economist may be permitted to comment on it with a few words. Should one, as Malthus, advocate further postponement of marriage, further reduction of nuptiality, and the almost inescapable consequence: an increased number of illegitimate births, increased immorality and prostitution? Hardly. On the contrary, in this respect a call for a better, more natural, and more humane way of life is irrefutable. But then there is no other choice besides the neomalthusian programme: early marriage but few children —on average 2–3 to a family—and, for the rest, voluntary sterility.[2]

Malthus took a negative view of what later come to be called the neomalthusian proposals, but more as a clergyman than as a social reformer. Against the natural objection that his own insistence on absolute abstinence during the major part of life would be difficult for many people, Malthus only has the rather unsatisfactory reply that he does not expect it. He only remarks that in social affairs the fulfilment of one duty, in this case the postponement

---

[1] Many scientists have lately begun to insist that individuals with congenital diseases, psychic and physical degenerates, should be morally obliged or otherwise prevented, in some cases incapacitated, from reproduction (a minor and harmless operation is said to be adequate) and also that those who are mentally and bodily best equipped should if necessary be supported in their efforts to create a family. This is the principal task of modern so-called racial hygiene. For my own part, I remain somewhat hesitant before these suggestions— except possibly in certain extreme cases—as long as research on the laws of genetics, especially in the psychic area, has not advanced farther than seems to be the case at present.

[2] As the group of women in the age 25–35 (in which fertility is concentrated) is about 37,000, it follows from what has been said that three children per mother is at present more than sufficient for the maintenance of the population. If mortality in younger years continues to decline in the same gratifying manner as in recent years, the proper average would even more approximate two children per woman and thereby, as far as I can see, also per family.

Professor Fahlbeck says that this average, especially if it is to apply to those families that have any children at all, is far too small, as many women remain unmarried and many marriages infertile, but he neglects, I think, the fact that both these circumstances are a condition of the present economic and social conditions which would be remedied by reduced fertility. There is no other decisive obstacle for all women (under favourable economic circumstances) to enter into marriage than their present excess numbers, which, as we have seen, is soon likely to disappear. As for marital sterility, it is well known to be frequently related to male venereal disease, according to some scholars in the majority of cases. This cause would also disappear, as soon as marriages were entered into at sufficiently early years, and it is presumably not beyond the realm of possibility that other causes of sterility could also be identified and cured by medical science. In addition, according to my conviction it would be desirable for our country to reduce its population significantly. In present circumstances, one could therefore justifiably recommend the two-child system, even in its strictest form, as a general rule of life in our country.

of marriage, will often be easier to the same extent that another duty, extra-marital abstinence, is left unfulfilled, and that although a human judge must demand the fulfilment of both duties, the heavenly judge who is able to weigh the temptation against the crime might pronounce a milder verdict.

That latter-day social reformers have not been able to stop at this half-way house is quite clear. All those who have recently argued for fertility reduction have also without exception been neomalthusians. The reception which at first was meted out to the preachers of these doctrines has not been gentle. Rodbertus' friend, von Kirchmann, the lawyer to whom he addressed his "Social Letters" was in the beginning of the 1860s deposed from a high judgeship without pension after having lectured on population to the workers of Berlin. Later than that, Charles Bradlaugh was on account of his neomalthusian views long refused his seat and voice in the British Parliament and once literally thrown out, not to mention much other public and private persecution. Yet public opinion in this matter has undergone a fundamental change. One indication is the position that Adolf Wagner has taken on neomalthusianism in the third edition of his *Grundlegung* (p. 462) and, even more unreservedly, the well-known Dutch statesman and economist N. G. Pierson (*Leerboek der staathuishoudkunde*, Bd. 2, s. 102 ff.). Among influential people in Scandinavia who have expressed themselves in the same spirit one could cite several medical authorities, and also the Danish philosopher Höffding.[1]

But from a physiological and technical point of view the problem cannot be said to have been satisfactorily solved. Most of the proposed methods are uncertain and rather crude. It would be desirable that medical experts directed their attention more to this problem than they have done. What is certain is that there is no area to which anatomic, physiological or gynaecological students could extend their researches that would be of greater significance from a social point of view.

---

[1] Even Professor Fahlbeck does not, as far as I have been able to find, reject neomalthusian methods, to the extent that a reduction of fertility would at all become necessary.

GPSR Compliance

The European Union's (EU) General Product Safety Regulation (GPSR) is a set of rules that requires consumer products to be safe and our obligations to ensure this.

If you have any concerns about our products, you can contact us on

ProductSafety@springernature.com

In case Publisher is established outside the EU, the EU authorized representative is:

Springer Nature Customer Service Center GmbH
Europaplatz 3
69115 Heidelberg, Germany

www.ingramcontent.com/pod-product-compliance
Lightning Source LLC
Chambersburg PA
CBHW071721100426
42873CB00016B/359